MACMILLAN READERS

INTERMEDIATE LEVEL

HELEN FIELDING

Bridget Jones's Diary

Retold by Anne Collins

MACMILLAN

MACMILLAN READERS

INTERMEDIATE LEVEL

Founding Editor: John Milne

The Macmillan Readers provide a choice of enjoyable reading materials for learners of English. The series is published at six levels – Starter, Beginner, Elementary, Pre-intermediate, Intermediate and Upper.

Level Control

Information, structure and vocabulary are controlled to suit the students' ability at each level.

The number of words at each level:

Starter	about 300 basic words
Beginner	about 600 basic words
Elementary	about 1100 basic words
Pre-intermediate	about 1400 basic words
Intermediate	about 1600 basic words
Upper	about 2200 basic words

Vocabulary

Some difficult words and phrases in this book are important for understanding the story. Some of these words are explained in the story, some are shown in the pictures, and others are marked with a number like this: ...[3]. Words with a number are explained in the Glossary at the end of the book.

Answer Keys

Answer Keys for the *Points for Understanding* and *Exercises* sections can be found at www.macmillanenglish.com/readers.

Contents

A Note About the Author

Helen Fielding was born on 19 February, 1958, in Yorkshire in the north of England. She went to Wakefield Girls' High School and then studied English at St Anne's College at the University of Oxford. She worked for many years in London as a newspaper and television journalist, travelling to Africa, India and Central America. During this time, she wrote her first novel, *Cause Celeb*, published in 1994, which was set in Africa.

In 1995, Helen was asked by the British newspaper, *The Independent*, to write a newspaper column about herself. But she preferred to write about a fictional woman instead. So she created the character of Bridget Jones – a single career woman in her thirties whose main goals in life are to lose weight and attract a man.

Many single women in their thirties identified[1] with Bridget. Nobody had written about their lives in such an honest and funny way before. Bridget was not a beautiful film heroine[2], but a likeable, ordinary woman with real-life problems. Helen's column became very popular and was turned into a book, *Bridget Jones's Diary*, which was published in 1996. The sequel – the book which follows it – *Bridget Jones: The Edge of Reason* was published in 1999. Both books became best-sellers and have been made into highly successful films.

Helen Fielding is a very funny writer. In 2003, she was listed in *The Observer* newspaper as one of the fifty funniest people in British comedy. Many other comedy writers are her friends.

Helen has written another novel, *Olivia Joules and the Overactive Imagination* (2003), and she co-wrote the screenplays for the two Bridget Jones films. Today she works full-time as a novelist and screenwriter, and lives in London and Los Angeles.

Bridget Jones was a great success because Helen Fielding wrote about a subject which not many other writers had written about before. She showed women that there is nothing wrong with being single. They shouldn't worry about it, but should enjoy life and have fun. Some people think that Helen Fielding is Bridget Jones and is writing about her own life. But this is not true. Helen says she wrote *Bridget Jones* as a way of making herself laugh. Many of the ideas in the book have come from her friends. She has succeeded well in making many other people laugh too.

A Note About the Story

Helen Fielding said that she got the idea for *Bridget Jones* from Jane Austen's famous novel, *Pride and Prejudice*. Although *Pride and Prejudice* was published in 1813, there are many similarities with *Bridget Jones*. Both plots centre round the problems of young women trying to attract a man. Like Elizabeth, the heroine of *Pride and Prejudice*, Bridget is attracted to a charming man who is wrong for her. But in the end, both heroines find true love.

Bridget Jones is a very warm, funny story. It is written as a diary, and takes place over one year of Bridget's life. So much of the story is told through Bridget's inner thoughts. The book is easy to read because we feel that Bridget is talking to us, and that we know her.

Bridget has a flat and a job in London. She works in the publicity department of a publishing company. She has three very good friends, whom she meets regularly for meals and drinks. The four friends support each other when they have emotional problems. Bridget has other friends as well, both married and single. But her big worry is that she has no boyfriend. She is afraid of never meeting the right man, and ending up alone.

Bridget is sure that she is very unattractive and is constantly trying to lose weight. She is always trying to eat and drink as few calories as possible. She thinks that men don't like her because she is too fat. But although she wants to attract a man, she still smokes, drinks and eats a lot! She also does foolish things, like getting drunk and having an affair[3] with her boss. And she is terrible at cooking.

Bridget is a very likeable character and women can easily identify with her problems. For example, many single women in their thirties have friends like Bridget's, who tell them that they must get married and have children before they get too old. But Bridget's experiences show us that married life brings problems too. The husband of one of Bridget's friends has an affair, and Bridget's own mother leaves her father.

Bridget was played brilliantly in both Bridget Jones films by Renée Zellweger, who is not British, but Texan! The main male characters were played by Colin Firth and Hugh Grant.

Cultural References

Bridget's flat is in South London. She lives the typical life of a young British career woman in her thirties, with a job and a car. She is not rich, but she has enough money to enjoy herself and go out for drinks and meals with her friends.

There are many references to well-known London restaurants, shops and other places in the story. For example, Debenhams, Café Rouge and Harvey Nichols. Bridget's boss, Perpetua, is a 'Sloane' – a rich and confident person from the area round Sloane Square in London's Chelsea. There is a reference to British cooking too. Bridget tries to cook for her friends, and decides to make shepherd's pie – a popular dish with meat and potatoes.

Bridget's parents have a typical British middle-class lifestyle. They live in a small village which is two hours' drive from London. Sometimes Bridget is invited to social events at her parents' friends' houses. Every New Year's Day, her mother's friend Una invites her friends over for a Turkey Lunch. Bridget meets the rich and divorced[4] Mark Darcy at this lunch, and this is where the story begins...

Stone – a unit for measuring weight in the UK containing 14 pounds. 1 stone = 6.35 kilograms. Bridget usually weighs around 9 stone. 9 stone = 57 kilograms.
Alcoholic units – used for measuring the amount of alcohol that people drink. 1 unit = 1 small glass of wine. Doctors in the

UK advise that women should not drink more than 14 units of alcohol in one week and men should not drink more than 21 units.

Calorie – a unit for measuring how much energy you get from food or drink. Doctors in the UK advise that women should not have more than 2000 calories a day and men should not have more than 2500.

The People in This Story

Bridget Jones

Mark Darcy

Daniel Cleaver

Jude

Shazzer

Tom

Magda

Jeremy

Bridget's mum

Bridget's dad

Julio

Una Alconbury

Geoffrey Alconbury

1

January: A Very Bad Start

New Year's Resolutions[5]

These are the things I decided I would do this year.

1. Stop smoking.
2. Develop a mature[6] relationship with an adult man.
3. Go to the gym.
4. Be kinder and help others more.

Sunday 1 January

Weight 9st 3, alcohol units 14, cigarettes 22, calories 5424.

Noon. London: my flat. Ugh! I've got to drive to Una and Geoffrey Alconbury's New Year's Day Turkey Lunch. Una and Geoffrey Alconbury are my parents' best friends and they have known me since I was a small child.

I'm not a child any more – I'm in my thirties with a flat and a job in London. But every year my mother makes me go to Una and Geoffrey Alconbury's New Year's Day Turkey Lunch. She usually tries to introduce me to a man she thinks would be a good boyfriend for me. But she always chooses the most awful men.

This year, for weeks before New Year's Day, my mother had talked about Mark Darcy. 'Do you remember Malcolm and Elaine Darcy, darling?' she kept saying. 'They're bringing their son Mark with them to Una's New Year's Day Turkey Lunch. He's a top lawyer – just back from America. He's just got divorced.'

I don't know why my mother didn't just say openly, 'Darling, Mark Darcy would make a very good boyfriend for you. He's *very* rich.'

11.45 p.m. Ugh! The first day of New Year has been awful. I took the wrong road on the way to the Alconburys' so I got lost and arrived very late.

'Bridget! Happy New Year!' said Geoffrey Alconbury. He gave me a huge hug[7]. 'Come on, let's get you a drink. How's your love-life?'

'Fine,' I said in an embarrassed sort of way.

'So you *still* haven't got a boyfriend!' said Geoffrey in a loud voice.

'If you don't hurry up and get married soon, you'll be too old to have children,' said Una, his wife. 'Come along and meet Mark.'

The rich, divorced Mark was standing with his back to us. He was quite tall and was looking at the books on the Alconburys' bookshelves.

'Mark!' said Una. 'I've got someone nice for you to meet.'

Mark Darcy turned round, and I saw that he was wearing a jumper with a pattern of yellow and blue diamonds on the front. It was awful.

'Mark, this is Colin and Pam's daughter, Bridget,' said Una. 'Bridget works in publishing, don't you, Bridget? Well, I'll leave you two young people together.' She went away quickly.

For a moment neither of us spoke.

'Um ... Have you been staying with your parents over New Year?' I asked him.

'Yes,' he said eagerly[8]. 'You too?'

'Yes. No. I was at a party in London last night,' I replied. Suddenly I started talking very quickly – too quickly. But I couldn't stop. Mark Darcy was looking at me with a look of horror on his face.

'Maybe you should get something to eat,' he said, and went away. Everyone was staring at me. I knew they were thinking, 'So that's why Bridget isn't married. She talks too much and is very unattractive to men.'

Mark Darcy was looking at me with a look of horror on his face.

Later, Una brought Mark over to me. 'Mark,' she said, 'you must take Bridget's telephone number, then you can get in touch when you're in London.'

I turned bright red. Now Mark would think I had told Una to say that.

'I'm sure Bridget's life in London is quite full enough already, Mrs Alconbury,' Mark replied.

I felt annoyed. I didn't want Mark to have my telephone number. But I didn't want everyone at the party to know that he didn't want it.

2 a.m. Oh, why am I so unattractive? Why? I hate New Year. I hate everyone – except Daniel Cleaver.

Tuesday 3 January

Weight 9st 4, alcohol units 6 (excellent), cigarettes 23, calories 2472.

9 a.m. Ugh! I cannot face[9] the thought of going to work. The only good thing about going to work is the thought of seeing Daniel again.

10 p.m. Ugh! Perpetua – who thinks she's my boss – talked for hours to her friends on the phone about the property she is buying with her rich boyfriend, Hugo. Perpetua was wearing a tight red skirt, which made her bottom[10] look very big.

But Perpetua doesn't care about how she looks. Perpetua is a Sloane, which means she is not only rich, but also very confident. I wish I could be like that.

Mmmm. I've been thinking about Daniel Cleaver. He asked me if I got anything nice for Christmas in a rather flirty way. I wonder if he's attracted to me. I think I might wear my short black skirt tomorrow.

Wednesday 4 January

Weight 9st 5, alcohol units 5, cigarettes 20, calories 700 (very good).

4 p.m. My friend Jude just rang up in tears because her boyfriend, Richard, has told her he doesn't want to see her any more. Jude's friends all call him 'Vile Richard' because he is *so* horrible. He thought she was getting too serious about their relationship because she asked him to go on holiday with her.

I immediately called Sharon (Shazzer), our other friend, and we arranged to meet Jude at 6.30 in Café Rouge.

11 p.m. Shazzer, who doesn't have a very high opinion[11] of men, gave us her ideas on Richard. And everyone else in Café Rouge heard.

'How *dare*[12] he say you were getting too serious about him?' she shouted. 'What is he *talking* about?'

I thought about Daniel Cleaver. 'Not all men are like Richard,' I said.

'Yes, but should I call Richard or not?' asked Jude.

'No,' said Sharon, just as I was saying, 'Yes.'

Thursday 5 January

Weight 9st 3 (excellent), alcohol units 6, cigarettes 12, calories 1258.

11 a.m. Office. Oh my God. Daniel Cleaver just sent me a message. I was sitting at my computer when New Mail suddenly flashed[13] up on my screen.

> Message Jones
> You appear to have forgotten your skirt.
> Cleave

Daniel Cleaver is flirting with me! I've never sent him a message before but I'm going to send him a funny one now.

Message Cleave
Sir, I am shocked by your message. My skirt is short, but it does exist.
Jones

Noon. Oh God. Daniel has not replied. Maybe he was being serious about my skirt.

12.10 p.m. Maybe he hasn't got my message yet.

12.15 p.m. Hah. Daniel is in a meeting with Simon from the Marketing Department. Aha. New Mail.

Message Jones
Your skirt is clearly absent[14]. Is skirt off sick?
Cleave

Just sending back:

Message Cleave
Skirt is neither sick nor abscent.
Jones

Oh dear. This was the return message.

Message Jones
'Absent', Jones, not 'abscent'. Try using a computer spell-check.
Cleave

Daniel walked past with Simon from Marketing and gave my skirt a very sexy look. I must try and improve my spelling.

Friday 6 January

5.45 p.m. I could not be happier. Daniel's last message read:

> Message Jones
> I wish to send flowers to your skirt over the weekend.
> Please give me your home telephone number.
> Cleave

Yesssss! Daniel Cleaver wants my phone no. Marvellous[15]!

Sunday 8 January

Weight 9st 2 (good, but what's the point?[16]), alcohol units 2 (excellent), cigarettes 7, calories 3100 (poor).

2 p.m. Oh God, why am I so unattractive? I've spent two days staring at the phone and waiting for Daniel to call.

8 p.m. The phone rang, but it was my friend Tom. Tom helps me a lot. He listened patiently while I told him first about Mark Darcy and then about Daniel. Then Tom said, 'Mark Darcy? But isn't he that famous human rights[17] lawyer?'

Monday 9 January

Weight 9st 2, alcohol units 4, cigarettes 29, calories 770.

It was a terrible day in the office. I watched the door for Daniel all morning.

Then Perpetua suddenly shouted into the phone: 'Daniel? He's gone to a meeting in Croydon. He'll be in tomorrow.' She banged down the phone and said, 'God, why are all these girls calling Daniel?'

When I went home that evening, in a mad moment I left a message on Daniel's answer-phone. I said, 'Hi, it's Jones here. I was just wondering if you wanted to meet to talk about the skirt.'

As soon as I put the phone down, I realised I had made a big mistake.

Tuesday 10 January

Weight 9st 1, alcohol units 2, cigarettes 0, calories 998 (excellent).

I crept into the office feeling really embarrassed about the message. Then Daniel appeared looking very sexy. Suddenly `New Mail` flashed up on my computer screen.

```
Message Jones
Thanks for your phone call.
Cleave
```

I sent back:

```
Message Cleave
Please shut up. I am very busy and important.
Jones
```

And after a few minutes more, he replied. Finally he suggested a date for Sunday night, and I accepted.

Sunday 15 January

Weight 9st (excellent), alcohol units 0, cigarettes 29 (very bad), calories 3879 (awful), negative thoughts 942.

6 p.m. I am completely exhausted[18] by getting ready for my date with Daniel. It has taken all day. Being a woman is worse than being a farmer. There's so much preparation and harvesting[19] to do.

7 p.m. I cannot believe this has happened. I was completing the final farming touches to my face and body, when I noticed the answer-phone light was flashing. It was Daniel.

'Look, Jones, I'm really sorry. I think I'm going to have to cancel tonight. I've got a presentation at ten in the morning.'

I cannot believe it. I've wasted the whole day.

9 p.m. Still, Daniel *is* in a top job. Maybe he didn't want to come on a first date worrying about work.

11 p.m. Humph[20]. He's probably out with someone thinner than I am.

5 a.m. What's wrong with me? I *hate* Daniel Cleaver.

Monday 16 January

Weight 9st 2 (from where? Why?), alcohol units 0, cigarettes 20, calories 1500, positive thoughts 0.

10.30 a.m. Daniel is still in his meeting. Maybe he was telling the truth.

1 p.m. I just saw Daniel leaving for lunch. He has not sent me any messages. I feel very depressed.

11.50 p.m. I just had dinner with Tom on the 5th floor at Harvey Nichols. I wanted to talk about Daniel but Tom talked all the time about someone new he's met – a film-maker.

Tuesday 24 January

Today was wonderful. At 5.30, Daniel sat down on the edge of my desk, took out his diary and whispered, 'What are you doing on Friday?'

Friday 27 January

Weight 9st 3, alcohol units 8, cigarettes 400 (feels like), calories 875.

Huh. We had a dream date at a little Italian restaurant near Daniel's flat.

After dinner, we went back to Daniel's flat. As soon as we were inside, he started to try and take off my skirt. Then he whispered, 'This is just a bit of fun, OK? I don't think we should start a relationship with each other.' But I immediately felt angry with him.

'That is such rubbish!' I said. 'You want me to sleep with you, but you don't want to have a relationship? I am not interested in emotional cowards[21]. Goodbye.' Then I walked out of the door.

I did the right thing. But now I feel depressed. I am afraid of one day being found dead in my flat, all alone, half-eaten by an animal.

2

February: Valentine's Day[22] Blues

Wednesday 1 February

Weight 9st, alcohol units 9, cigarettes 28, calories 3826.

On Sunday, I went for lunch at my parents' house. My mother had just returned from a week's holiday in Portugal with Una Alconbury. When I was about to leave, my Dad came out to the garage.

'Have you noticed anything unusual about your mother?' he asked.

'No,' I replied. 'Except that she looks very well after her holiday.'

I found out from Perpetua that Daniel's gone to New York. He's probably got a cool[23] American girlfriend there.

I have to go to a dinner party tonight at the house of my married friends, Magda and Jeremy. Most of their friends are other married couples. I call them the 'Smug[24] Marrieds' because they think their lives are better than those of single people.

11.45 p.m. Oh God. The party was me, four married couples and Jeremy's brother. (He's awful – fat with a red face.)

'So,' shouted Jeremy's friend, Cosmo. 'How's your love-life?'

'Yes, why aren't you married yet, Bridget?' said Cosmo's wife, Woney.

Because I don't want to be like you, you fat boring Sloane cow, I thought.

'It's very difficult to find a good husband once you get past a certain age,' said another friend of Jeremy's.

'Yes, why aren't you married yet, Bridget?'
said Cosmo's wife, Woney.

'Exactly. All the decent[25] men have been taken,' said Cosmo. 'My office is full of single girls over thirty who can't get a boyfriend.'

'Sorry about those people,' said Magda later, who knew how embarrassed I was feeling. 'Will you be OK getting home?'

'Do you want a lift?' said Jeremy's brother.

'Actually, I'm going on to a nightclub,' I said happily, hurrying out into the street. 'Thanks for a super evening.'

Then I got into a taxi and burst[26] into tears.

Sunday 5 February

Daniel still hasn't been in touch. There's only a week to go until Valentine's Day. I'm sure I won't get any cards.

I think I'll go and see Mum and Dad again. I'll feel like a caring angel and won't think about Daniel. I'm worried about Dad.

2 p.m. I rang Dad, but his voice sounded very strange.

'Bridget, look, your mother and I are having some problems. Can we ring you later in the week?'

Problems? What problems? But Dad wouldn't tell me anything more.

Monday 6 February

Weight 8st 12 (internal weight has completely vanished[27] – mystery), alcohol units 1, cigarettes 9, calories 1800.

Daniel will be back from New York today. I shall be very cool[28]. I am not going to send him any messages or take any notice of him.

9.30 a.m. Humph. Daniel does not seem to be here yet.

9.36 a.m. Oh God, oh God. Maybe Daniel's fallen in love with someone in New York. Or gone to Las Vegas and got married.

10.05 a.m. I saw Daniel standing at the photocopier with Simon from Marketing. He looked very well and healthy. As I passed he looked at my skirt and gave me a huge grin[29].

10.30 a.m. New Mail flashed up on my screen.

> Message Jones
> Unfriendly cow.
> Cleave

I laughed. But I am not going to send him a message back.

10.35 a.m. It seems rude not to reply though.

10.47 a.m. I'll just send him a tiny friendly little message.

10 p.m. Daniel and I messaged each other all day. But there is no way I am going to sleep with him.

I called Mum and Dad again tonight but no one answered. It's very weird[30].

Thursday 9 February

Weight 9st 2, alcohol units 4, cigarettes 12, calories 2845 (I need extra fat because it's winter and I'm very cold).

9 p.m. It's snowing. I like this winter weather. This is the third time I have called Mum and Dad this week and got no reply.

9.15 p.m. I just called Mum and Dad, letting the phone ring twenty times. Finally Mum answered sounding very strange and saying she couldn't talk now but would call me at the weekend.

Saturday 11 February

Weight 8st 13, alcohol units 4, cigarettes 18, calories 1467.

My dad left a message on my answer-phone, asking if I would meet him for lunch on Sunday. I was very shocked. My dad never comes to London on Sundays. I went out to the shop round the corner. When I got back, there was a message on my answer-phone from Mum. She is also coming for lunch tomorrow.

Sunday 12 February

Weight 8st 13, alcohol units 5, cigarettes 23 (not surprising), calories 1647.

11 a.m. Oh God, I can't have them both coming for lunch.

12.05 p.m. Mum called. I told her that Dad was coming for lunch. 'Let *him* come then,' she said. 'I'll be all right here on my own.'

At 2 o'clock Dad arrived. He sat down on the sofa and started to cry.

'She's been like this ever since she went to Portugal with Una,' he said, wiping his cheek. 'When she got back, she said she wanted to be paid for doing the housework, and she'd wasted her life being our servant[31].'

Monday 13 February

Oh God. Tomorrow is February the 14th, Valentine's Day. But everyone knows romance does not work. Valentine's Day has no meaning. It's just a commercial occasion[32] when companies which produce cards and chocolates make lots of money. I don't care about it. It's silly.

Tuesday 14 February

8 a.m. Oh good. It's Valentine's Day. I wonder if the post has come yet. Maybe there will be a card from Daniel.

There was a bunch of roses in the hallway. I rushed down and picked them up. Then Vanessa, the girl who lives in the flat downstairs, came out.

'Ooh, they look nice,' she said. 'Who are they from?'

'I don't know,' I said, looking down at the card. 'Ah ... they're for you.'

I got into the office to find that Perpetua had a huge bunch of flowers on her desk from her boyfriend, Hugo.

'How many Valentines did you get, Bridget?' she shouted in a loud voice.

'Valentine's Day is silly and doesn't mean anything,' I replied. 'It's just a commercial occasion.'

Just then I noticed Daniel across the room. He was listening to us and laughing.

Wednesday 15 February

I had an unexpected surprise. I was just leaving my flat for work when I noticed there was a pink envelope on the hall table – a late Valentine – which said, 'To the dark beauty'. For a moment I was excited, imagining it was for me. Then I remembered that Vanessa is dark-haired. Humph.

9 p.m. I just got back and the card is still there.

10 p.m. It's still there.

11 p.m. I can't believe it. The card is still there.

Thursday 16 February

Weight 8st 12 (weight loss because I was going up and down the stairs), alcohol units 0 (excellent), cigarettes 5, calories 2452.

The card is still there! Vanessa and I are both too polite to take it.

Friday 17 February

Weight 8st 12, alcohol units 1, cigarettes 2, calories 3241, checks on card 12.

9 a.m. The card is still there.

9 p.m. It's still there.

9.30 p.m. It's still there. I knocked on Vanessa's door. 'I think this must be for you,' I said, holding out the card.

'Oh, I thought it must be for *you*,' she said.

We opened the card. Inside it said,

'*A piece of silly and meaningless commercialism for my darling little unfriendly cow.*'

I gave a scream of excitement. Daniel had sent me a Valentine's card!

Saturday 18 February

Weight 9st, alcohol units 4, cigarettes 6, calories 2746, correct lottery numbers 2.

At last I've found out what the problem is with Mum and Dad.

Today Mum asked me to meet her for lunch in a department store. I asked her if she was seeing someone else.

'No. There is no one else,' she said, staring into the distance. 'But when your father retired[33], I realised that I've spent thirty-five years running his home and looking after him. You only get one life. I'm going to start looking after myself now.'

I went to pay the bill. Then I noticed a tall man with grey hair and a leather jacket. He was looking into the café and tapping[34] his watch. I turned round and saw my mother mouthing him the words, 'I won't be very long'.

After we said goodbye, I followed Mum. Soon she was in the perfume department with the grey-haired man, trying different perfumes. She was holding the bottles of perfume up for him to smell and laughing like a girl.

Sunday 19 February

Weight 8st 13 (only because of worry), alcohol units 2, cigarettes 7, calories 2100.

I called Mum to ask her about the man I saw her with.

'Oh, you must mean Julio,' she said in a nervous voice.

I had never heard of this Julio before. I guessed that she had met him in Portugal, before the trouble with Dad. I guessed that Julio *was* the reason for the trouble with Dad. I asked Mum if this was true.

'You're becoming very suspicious[35], darling,' she said. 'Julio – aha! – is only a friend. I just need some space.'

She then told me that, to give her space, Dad is moving into the Alconburys' flat at the bottom of their garden.

Tuesday 21 February

I'm very tired. Dad has started ringing up in the night, just to talk.

Wednesday 22 February

Weight 9st, alcohol units 2, cigarettes 19, fat units 8.

I have been so busy worrying about Mum and Dad, and so tired from Dad's phone calls, that I have not taken very much notice of Daniel. As a result, he has paid me a lot of attention[36].

Thursday 23 February

Weight 8st 13, alcohol units 2, cigarettes 17 (I'm nervous about tomorrow), calories 775.

8 p.m. Daniel has asked me to have dinner with him tomorrow. Yessss!

Saturday 25 February

Weight 8st 10 (sex is good for losing weight), alcohol units 0, cigarettes 0, calories 200 (the secret of not eating is to replace food with sex).

6 p.m. I am so happy. I've spent the day in a lovely dream. I had a wonderful sexy night with Daniel last night.

But I'm beginning to feel worried. What's going to happen now? Suddenly I realise I'm waiting for the phone again.

11 p.m. Oh God. Why hasn't Daniel rung? Are we going out now, or what?

Sunday 26 February

Weight 9st, alcohol units 5, cigarettes 23, calories 3856 (to try and forget how unhappy I am).

I awoke, alone, to find myself imagining my mother with Julio. I felt full of jealousy about being in bed alone on Sunday morning while my mother is probably having a lot of fun.

3

March: Birthday Panic[37]

Saturday 4 March

Weight 9st (what is the point of dieting when I end up exactly the same weight at the start of March as at the start of February? Huh. I am going to stop getting weighed – there's no point).

My mother came into my flat this morning with a pile of carrier bags.

'Darling, can I leave these here for a few hours?' she cried, going into my bedroom. She sat down in front of the mirror and put on her eye make-up. She looked beautiful. Her skin was clear and her hair was shining.

'I'm having lunch with a man from the tax office today,' she said. 'I rang up to ask the tax office how to fill in my tax form, and he helped me. Then he asked me to have lunch with him.'

'What about Julio?' I said.

'Just because I'm 'friends' with Julio doesn't mean I can't have other friends,' she said sweetly. 'Anyway, I must rush. I'm meeting him at Debenhams' coffee shop at one fifteen.'

I know what my mother's secret is – she's discovered she has power. She has power over Dad: he wants her back. She has power over Julio and the tax man. Everyone wants her. So I have to find someone to have power over too.

I am so depressed. Daniel has been very friendly all week. But he hasn't said anything about 'us'. Perhaps he thinks it's normal to sleep with one of your colleagues without asking to see her again.

At 4.15 on Friday evening Shazzer rang me in the office. 'Are you coming out with me and Jude tomorrow?' she asked.

'Er ...' I didn't know what to say. I was thinking, *Surely Daniel will ask to see me this weekend before he leaves the office?*

'Call me if he doesn't ask,' said Shazzer after a pause.

At 5.45 I saw Daniel leaving the office. He smiled, nodded at the computer screen and left quickly. I looked at the computer. New Mail was flashing.

> Message Jones
> Have a good weekend.
> Cleave

I felt miserable. I picked up the phone and called Shazzer.

'What time are we meeting tomorrow?' I asked.

'Eight thirty,' she replied. 'At Café Rouge. Don't waste your time thinking about him.'

Sunday 5 March

Noon. We had good fun last night but I'm confused. I told Shazzer and Jude that I had slept with Daniel but then he hadn't asked to see me again. They both had different advice. Jude said Daniel was probably worried about work, so I should give him a chance. Shazzer said he had behaved very badly and I should tell him what I think of him. Hmmm.

Monday 6 March

Weight 8st 12 (I have realised the secret of dieting is not weighing oneself).

11 a.m. Office. I'm completely exhausted. Last night I was just lying in a nice hot bath when the doorbell rang. It was my mother, crying.

'I want a career,' she said. 'I haven't got anything of my own.'

By the time my mother left it was after ten, so I called Tom. I told him that Daniel had not called me all weekend. Tom said I should behave like a cool ice-queen[38]. If I really want Daniel and want to win his heart, I should be as cold and distant towards him as possible.

I finally went to bed, but I was woken three times in the night by phone calls from Dad.

Monday 6 March

Tom was right. The way to a man's heart is not through beauty, food or sex, but the ability to seem not very interested in him.

I took no notice of Daniel all day and pretended to be busy with my work. New Mail kept flashing on my computer screen but I didn't open it. At the end of the day, Daniel walked past my desk, stopped for a moment and murmured, 'Jones, you gorgeous[39] creature. Why are you ignoring[40] me?'

Tuesday 7 March

Weight 9st 4, 2, or 5??? alcohol units 0, cigarettes 20, calories 1500.

I am very depressed about my weight. I keep trying different diets but I never lose any weight. I put weight on instead. How can that happen?

5 a.m. Oh God, I'm so unhappy about Daniel. I love him.

Wednesday 15 March

Weight 9st, alcohol units 5, cigarettes 14, calories 1795.

I am worried about how to celebrate my birthday. Perhaps I could invite my friends for dinner? But then I would have to spend my birthday cooking. We could go out for a meal, but I can't afford to pay for everyone. Oh God. What shall I do?

Midnight. I have had a very good idea about my birthday. I will ask everyone to come for drinks. If they want to go to dinner afterwards, they can.

Thursday 16 March

Weight 9st 1, alcohol units 2, cigarettes 3, calories 2140 (but mainly fruit), minutes spent doing party guest list 237 (bad).

I wrote down a list of people to invite to my drinks party.

Me	
Sharon	
Jude	Vile Richard
Tom	
Magda	Jeremy
Simon	
Rebecca	Martin (very boring)
Woney	Cosmo
Joanna	
Daniel?	Perpetua? (eek) and Hugo?

Oh no. That's too many people. What am I going to do?

Friday 17 March

I just called Tom who says, 'It is *your* birthday and you should invite only who you want.'

So I am just going to ask the following people:

Sharon
Jude
Tom
Magda and Jeremy

– and cook supper for everyone myself.

When I told Jude who was coming she said, 'Can we bring our partners?' which means Vile Richard.

Next, Shazzer rang. 'I hope I haven't said anything wrong,' she said. 'I just saw Rebecca and asked her if she was coming to your birthday.'

Oh no, now I'll have to ask Rebecca and Martin, her boring boyfriend. And now I've said I'm cooking. I can't suddenly change my mind and say we're going out to a restaurant. People will think I'm lazy.

In the end, I realised I was going to spend my birthday cooking food for fifteen people.

Saturday 18 March

Weight 8st 13, alcohol units 4, cigarettes 23 (very bad as I smoked them in two hours), calories 3827 (awful).

2 p.m. My mother burst into my flat, looking very happy. 'Darling, what's the matter?' she asked. 'Have you had a bad week? You look dreadful. Anyway, guess what's happened?'

'What?' I said crossly.

'I've got a job as a TV presenter.'

Sunday 19 March

Weight 8st 12, alcohol units 3, cigarettes 10, calories 2465 (but mainly chocolate).

I've realised it is very wrong and selfish of me to not want to cook dinner for my friends. These people are like a big warm family. I am going to cook shepherd's pie for them all – British Home Cooking.

Monday 20 March

Weight 9st, alcohol units 4, cigarettes 27 (but I'm giving them up soon), calories 2455.

I've decided to serve the shepherd's pie with a special salad and a nice dessert. I haven't made the dessert before, but I am sure it will be easy. I expect that I will become known as a brilliant cook and hostess[41].

Tuesday 21 March: Birthday

Weight 9st, alcohol units 9, cigarettes 42, calories 4295 (but it IS *my birthday!)*

6.30 p.m. I cannot go on. I have just stepped in a pan of shepherd's pie which was on the kitchen floor. It is already 6.30 and I still have to go out and buy the ingredients to make the dessert.

7.15 p.m. I just got back from the shop and realised I have forgotten the butter.

7.35 p.m. The shepherd's pie is still in pans all over the kitchen floor and I have not yet washed my hair.

7.40 p.m. Oh my God. I just looked for the milk and realised that I've left the carrier bag behind in the shop. That means … Oh God, and the olive oil … so I cannot make the salad.

7.55 p.m. Aargh. That's the doorbell. I am in my underwear with wet hair. I suddenly hate my guests. I just want to open the door and shout, 'Go away!'

2 a.m. I am feeling very happy. Magda, Tom, Sharon and Jude were at the door with a bottle of champagne. They told me to hurry up and get ready. While I dried my hair, they cleaned up the kitchen and threw away the shepherd's pie. Magda had booked a table at a restaurant and everyone was there, waiting

Magda, Tom, Sharon and Jude were at the door with a bottle of champagne.

with presents, planning to buy me dinner. Magda said they had a weird feeling that dinner at my flat would not work out. I love my friends.

4

April: Inner Poise[42]

Weight 9st, alcohol units 0 (marvellous), cigarettes 0, calories 2250.

I am trying to develop 'inner poise'. In other words, I'm trying to appear calm and relaxed. I keep repeating 'inner poise' to myself.

9 p.m. My father called. His voice sounded very strange.

'Bridget. Turn your television on to BBC1.'

I switched on my TV. It was an advertisement for a chat show[43]. Suddenly I saw my mother, with her face made-up and a new hairstyle. I was very shocked. One of the chat show hosts was talking.

'… and we'll be introducing our new presenter, Pam Jones,' he was saying. 'Pam is going to present our new series, *Suddenly Single*. Pam has recently become single herself.'

Dad was very upset. Mum hadn't even told him about the TV-presenting job. Poor Dad. I don't think he knows anything about Julio or the man from the tax office.

Thursday 6 April

Weight 8st 13, alcohol units 5 (Jude's fault), cigarettes 2 (that doesn't mean I've started smoking again), calories 1765.

I met Jude for a drink. Then I saw my friend Magda's husband, Jeremy, sitting in a quiet corner of the restaurant. I waved at him but when he saw me, he looked horrified. There was a woman with him. She was (a) not Magda (b) not yet thirty and (c) wearing an expensive suit which I have seen in a shop but couldn't afford to buy.

I walked towards Jeremy's table, but he started talking to the woman very fast. Then he looked up and smiled at me, as if to say, 'It's a business meeting.' I gave him a look which said 'I don't believe you', and walked on.

What should I do now? Magda is my friend. Should I tell her about Jeremy and this woman? Should I not tell Magda? Should I ring Jeremy and threaten to tell Magda unless he stops seeing this woman?

Finally I decided not to tell anyone.

Tuesday 11 April

Weight 8st 11, alcohol units 0, cigarettes 0.

Next week my company is publishing an important new book, *Kafka's Motorbike*. I have been invited to the party to celebrate the book's publication. Lots of top people from the publishing world will be there.

I'm scared about this party. I'm not very good at parties. But I have been reading a magazine article about how to behave at them.

When you are introducing people to each other, you should give each person some information about the other person. For example, 'This is John – he's from New Zealand and he enjoys windsurfing.'

You should go to a party with a clear aim – for example, to meet people who can help you in your career or to make friends with a particular person.

Monday 17 April

Weight 8st 12, alcohol units 0 (very good), cigarettes 0 (very good).

Right. Tomorrow is the *Kafka's Motorbike* party. Here are my aims for the party:

1. Not to get too drunk.
2. To meet people who will be able to help me in my career.

Hmmm. I'll think of some more aims later.

11 p.m. Right.

3. To use the social skills I learned about in the article.
4. ~~To make Daniel think I have inner poise so that he will flirt with me again. No. No.~~
4. ~~To meet and sleep with a sex-god.~~ No!
4. To make interesting contacts with people in the publishing world, and other professions in order to find a new career.

Oh God. I don't want to go to this party. I want to stay at home with a bottle of wine and watch television.

Tuesday 18 April

The party started badly. I could not see anyone that I knew. I got a drink then I saw Perpetua talking to a newspaper reporter. I went up to her, but she didn't introduce me to the reporter. Then I saw Simon from Marketing. I went to join him, but he was talking to a famous author, Julian Barnes.

'Did you want something, Bridget?' asked Simon.

'Ah! Yes!' I said, trying to think of something quickly.

'Yeees?' Simon and Julian Barnes both looked at me.

'Do you know where the toilets are?' I asked. Oh no. Why did I say that?

Julian Barnes smiled faintly.

'Ah,' he said. 'Actually, I think they're over there.'

'Thanks,' I said. I went out of the exit door and leaned against the wall. The party was not going very well for me. I breathed in deeply, whispered 'inner poise' to myself, and went back into the party. Perpetua was still standing by the door, talking to two of her awful friends, Piggy and Arabella.

'Oh, look, there's Mark,' said Piggy.

'Oh, yah,' said Arabella. 'He's left his wife, hasn't he?'

I looked up and saw a dark-haired man in a suit standing in front of me.

'Hello, Bridget,' he said. I opened my mouth with shock. It was Mark Darcy.

'Hello,' I said. Then I remembered the article and turned towards Perpetua.

'Mark. Perpetua is ... ' I began, and then paused.

'Yes?' said Mark.

' ... is my boss and is buying a flat in Fulham, and Mark is,' I said, turning to Perpetua, 'a top human-rights lawyer.'

'Oh, hello, Mark. I know *of* you, of course,' said Perpetua as if Mark was a member of the royal family.

'This is Natasha,' said Mark, introducing a tall, thin, attractive girl beside him. 'Natasha is a top lawyer who specialises in family law.'

Natasha, Perpetua and Arabella all started to talk together in loud voices.

Later I was putting on my coat when I felt someone's hands round my waist.

I turned round. 'Daniel!'

'Jones! Why are you leaving the party so early?' He leaned over and kissed me. 'Mmmmm, you smell nice.' Then he offered me a cigarette.

'No, thank you,' I said. I wished that Daniel wasn't so attractive. 'Have you been at the party? I didn't see you.'

'I know you didn't. But I saw you. You were talking to Mark Darcy.'

'How do you know Mark Darcy?' I was very surprised.

'I met him when we were both at Cambridge University. But I don't like him. How do you know him?'

'He's the son of friends of my parents,' I replied. 'I've known him since we were children.'

'Come on, Bridge,' said Daniel, leaning towards me. 'I need to talk to you.'

'No,' I said. 'I've got to meet someone.'

'What a pity,' he said. 'Well, see you on Monday.'

11 p.m. I just called Jude and told her about Daniel. Then I told her about Mark Darcy, who had turned up at the party looking rather attractive.

'Wait a minute,' said Jude. 'You don't mean *Mark* Darcy, do you? The lawyer?'

'Yes. What – do you know him?'

'Well, yes,' said Jude. 'I mean, my company's done some work with him. He's extremely nice and attractive.'

Friday 28 April

Alcohol units 14, cigarettes 64, calories 8400.

At 8.45 last night I was running the water for a bath when a car alarm started making a terrible noise. Then the doorbell rang. I picked up the entry phone and heard Magda's voice, saying loudly, 'Jeremy's having an affair.'

I rushed downstairs and found Magda outside crying. She was sitting in Jeremy's car, which was making a dreadful noise. The baby was sitting in the back of the car, screaming. Magda was looking for the switch to turn the car alarm off.

'Turn it off!' shouted someone from an upstairs window.

'I can't!' shouted Magda. She took out her mobile phone and screamed into it, 'Jeremy! I'm not coming back. Just tell me how to turn off the car alarm!'

I got into the car with Magda. We pulled all the switches, trying to turn off the car alarm. An angry crowd started to gather round the car. Then Jeremy roared up on his motorbike. But instead of turning off the alarm, he started trying to grab[44] the baby out of the back seat.

Dan, the Australian guy who lives below me, opened his window.

'Bridget!' he shouted. 'There's water pouring through my ceiling!'

'Oh no!'

I had forgotten to turn off the bath when I rushed outside to help Magda.

I ran upstairs but I had shut the door of my flat and the key was inside. Then Dan appeared in the hall. He opened the door of the flat using a credit card.

There was water everywhere. At last Dan managed to turn off the taps. Suddenly the car alarm stopped. I rushed to the window and saw Jeremy's car racing down the street, followed by Jeremy on his motor-bike.

After Dan left, the doorbell rang. I ignored it. It rang again – on and on without stopping. I picked it up.

'Darling,' said a drunken voice. I knew that voice. It was Daniel.

'Go away,' I said.

'No. Let me explain.'

'No.'

'Bridge … I want to come in. I love you.'

'Go away. You're drunk,' I said in the strongest voice I could manage.

'Jones?'

'What?'

'Can I use your toilet?'

Saturday 29 April

Alcohol units 12, cigarettes 57, calories 8489 (excellent!).

It's twenty-two hours later and Daniel is still here. We've eaten four pizzas and an Indian takeaway meal; we've smoked three

'Bridget!' Dan shouted. 'There's water pouring through my ceiling!'

packets of cigarettes and drunk three bottles of champagne. I am in love. I may also be:

a) Smoking thirty cigarettes a day.
b) Engaged.
c) Stupid.
d) Pregnant[45].

5

May: Mother-to-Be

Alcohol units 0, cigarettes 0, calories 4200 (but now I'm eating for two people).

I seriously think I am pregnant. How could Daniel and I have been so stupid and forgotten to be careful? This morning I definitely felt sick. But perhaps that was because I ate too many sweets and chocolate yesterday.

Perpetua was being very difficult in the office today. She talked for forty-five minutes to one of her friends about the flat she's buying with her boyfriend, Hugo. But I didn't care. I was dreaming about Daniel and our baby. I imagined Daniel carrying the baby … Daniel rushing home from work to see me and the baby.

But then Daniel appeared. He looked terrible. He stared at me in a very unfriendly way. Suddenly all my romantic dreams disappeared.

Wednesday 3 May

Weight 9st 2 (the baby is growing very fast), alcohol units 0, cigarettes 0, calories 3100 (but mainly potatoes).

Help! I really think I might be pregnant. Daniel ignored me all day on Monday and then at 6 p.m. he said, 'Listen, I'm going to be in Manchester till the end of the week. I'll see you on Saturday night, OK?'

He hasn't called me since. I am going to be a single mother.

Thursday 4 May

Weight 9st 3, alcohol units 0, cigarettes 0, potatoes 12.

This morning I went to the chemist to buy a pregnancy test. I took it back to the office and went to the ladies' toilets. After I had used the test, I saw a thin blue line appear. I nearly screamed. The blue line meant I was pregnant!

I went back to my computer but I couldn't concentrate[46]. Finally, I went outside to a phone box and called Shazzer. We arranged to meet in the Café Rouge in fifteen minutes.

When Shazzer arrived, I showed her the thin blue line on the pregnancy test.

'You silly girl,' she said. 'Didn't you read the instructions? If you're pregnant, *two* blue lines will appear. One line means you're *not* pregnant – you idiot[47].'

Friday 5 May

Weight 9st, alcohol units 6, cigarettes 25, calories 1890.

11.45 p.m. Daniel just called from Manchester.

'Have you had a good week?' he asked.

'Super, thanks,' I said brightly. I've read somewhere that the best gift a woman can give to a man is peace. So I'm not going to tell Daniel that I got upset because I thought I was pregnant.

We're seeing each other tomorrow night. Great!

Saturday 6 May

Weight 9st 1, alcohol units 6, cigarettes 25, calories 3800.

7 p.m. The weather is very hot. My body is twice as big as usual. I went shopping today and tried on a dress in the shop's changing room. The dress got stuck and I couldn't get it

The blue line meant I was pregnant!

off. A crowd of fifteen-year old girls were watching me and laughing.

Anyway, Daniel will be here soon. I think I'll just have a little drink first.

11.59 p.m. I'm in the kitchen having a cigarette. Daniel is asleep. Actually I think he's pretending to be asleep. It's been a very strange evening. Daniel didn't seem interested in sex at all. We sat watching television. Later, in bed, Daniel put on his reading glasses and read a book for twenty-five minutes. Then he switched off the light and went to sleep.

I preferred Daniel when he was always wanting sex with me.

Saturday 13 May

Weight 9st 1, cigarettes 7, calories 1145.

I had a really great evening last night. Sharon and Jude came round and brought wine and food with them, so I didn't have to do any cooking.

Jude was depressed because Vile Richard wants to end their relationship. 'How dare he treat you so badly?' shouted Sharon. 'Men are such rats[48]!'

Just then the doorbell rang.

'Oh, hello, darling,' said Daniel in a gentle, polite voice. 'I rang earlier and left a message on your answer-phone. I've been working late, but I so much wanted to see you. Can I come up?'

'All right, then,' I said crossly.

Then Daniel appeared, smiling in a loving way. He was holding three boxes of chocolates.

'I bought you all one of these,' he said, 'to eat with your coffee. Don't let me interrupt[49] your evening. I've done the shopping for the weekend.'

He took some bags from the supermarket into the kitchen and started putting everything away. Then he offered to drive the girls home. When they had gone, I ate my chocolates and thought about Daniel. He was pretending to be the perfect man!

When he came home, he ran up the stairs and carried me into the bedroom.

'You're lovely even when you're drunk,' he said.

Tuesday 17 May

Weight 9st 2, cigarettes 7 (very good), alcohol units 6.

Daniel is still being lovely. How could everyone have been so wrong about him? I keep dreaming about living with him and running along beaches together.

I'm just going to meet Magda.

11 p.m. Hmmm. I had supper with Magda, who is very depressed about Jeremy. She told me that her friend Woney had seen Jeremy with a girl in a club. Magda asked me if I knew anything about the girl, so I told her about the girl I had seen with Jeremy. It sounded like the same girl.

'You should enjoy being single while you can, Bridge,' said Magda. 'It's very hard work, staying at home and looking after kids. But Jeremy thinks my life is just a long holiday. And now he's dreaming about girls in clubs.'

Magda is so beautiful. I thought how difficult life is for us girls. We always want what we haven't got. I'm always thinking that my life is empty and useless. I don't have very much money and all I do is go out and get drunk with my friends every Saturday. Magda is married and lives in a beautiful house with her husband and two children. And she's telling me *I'm* lucky.

Friday 19 May

Weight 8st 12, alcohol units 4, cigarettes 21 (bad).

4.30 p.m. The phone rang while I was still at work. It was my mother.

'Hello, darling!' she said. 'Guess what? I've got the most marvellous opportunity[50] for you. You're going to be on television. I'm coming round to your place with the TV crew at ten o'clock tomorrow. The TV people want me to interview someone younger than I am for *Suddenly Single*.'

'I'm not Suddenly Single!' I shouted. 'I've got a boyfriend.'

'Oh, please, darling. I've told them I've found someone. Pleeeeeeease. I've never had a career all my life and now I'm getting old and I need something for myself,' she said, talking very fast.

'Well, won't the people notice I'm your daughter?'

I could hear her talking to someone in the background. Then she came back and said, 'We won't show your face. Oh, please, Bridget.'

The truth is that I've always secretly liked the idea of being on television.

Saturday 20 May

Weight 9st 3 (why? why? from where?), alcohol units 7, cigarettes 17.

Everything went wrong with the filming. The TV crew broke a lot of things in my apartment with their big heavy cameras. Three hours after they arrived, they had still not started filming. At last, at half-past one, Mother and I sat on the sofa together.

'And tell me,' she said in a caring, understanding voice I'd never heard before. 'When your husband left you, did you want to kill yourself?'

I stared at her, too shocked and angry to speak. What was she talking about? What husband?

'I mean, it must be a terrible time for you. You don't have a partner and you'll soon be too old to have children,' she said, kicking me under the table. I kicked her back and she let out a little noise.

'Don't you want a child?' she asked.

At that moment someone at the back of the room laughed loudly. I had forgotten that Daniel had stayed last night. He had been asleep in the bedroom.

'If Bridget had a child, she'd lose it,' he said, laughing loudly.

Sunday 21 May

My mum is not speaking to Daniel or me, because Daniel told the TV crew I was her daughter. Maybe she'll leave me alone now.

I'm really looking forward to the summer. It will be so lovely having a boyfriend when it is warm. We will be able to go on romantic minibreaks[51]. The thought of going away at weekends with Daniel makes me very happy.

6

June: Hah! Boyfriend

Weight 8st 13, alcohol units 5, cigarettes 25, calories 600, minutes spent looking at minibreaks 87.

The weather is very hot. I'm finding it impossible to concentrate on anything except being on lovely minibreaks with Daniel. I keep imagining us lying in grassy places, or by rivers, or having a drink and watching the sunset over the sea. I imagine us having dinner by candlelight in hotels in the country, and then making love all night.

Tomorrow I expect we will go to the park or out to a lovely pub in the country for lunch. It is marvellous having a boyfriend.

Sunday 4 June

7 p.m. Humph. Daniel has just gone home. I'm a bit fed up, actually. The weather was lovely and hot today, but Daniel did not want to go out or discuss minibreaks. He wanted to spend all afternoon with the curtains shut, watching cricket[52] on television.

Tuesday 6 June

Weight 9st 2, alcohol units 4, cigarettes 3 (very good), calories 1326, hours spent asleep 15 (but it's very hot).

I managed to persuade[53] Perpetua to let me stay at home today to work. I'm sure she only agreed because she wants to sunbathe too. I've got a lovely new minibreak brochure: 'The Top Country House Hotels of Britain.' Marvellous. I'm imagining sexy and romantic scenes with Daniel in all the bedrooms and dining-rooms.

11 a.m. Right. I'm going to concentrate on my work now.

11.35 a.m. I don't know why, but I've just started imagining that Daniel is having an affair with someone else. Am I taking our relationship too seriously? Is Daniel having an affair?

12.40 p.m. I'm very hot in my shorts and T-shirt. I think I'll change into a long dress.

1 p.m. Lunchtime! At last a bit of time off from work.

2 p.m. OK, so this afternoon I am really going to work. I'm very sleepy though. It's so hot. Maybe I'll just close my eyes for five minutes. Maybe I'll lie down on the bed.

7.30 p.m. Oh no! I've slept all afternoon.

Sunday 11 June

I've just wasted another Sunday, watching cricket on television with Daniel.

Everybody else is outside, enjoying the hot weather and having fun picnics in the park. But I'm stuck inside with the curtains closed, watching TV.

Sunday 18 June

Weight 8st 12, alcohol units 3, cigarettes 17.

This was the third Sunday I have spent watching cricket with Daniel. Suddenly I decided that I couldn't bear[54] it any more.

'Why can't we go on a minibreak?' I asked. 'Why? Why?'

'That's a good idea,' said Daniel. 'Why don't you book somewhere for next weekend? Book a nice country hotel. I'll pay.'

Wednesday 21 June

Weight 8st 11 (very good), alcohol units 1, cigarettes 2, minutes spent looking at minibreak brochures 237 (bad).

Daniel has refused to discuss the minibreak any more, or look at the brochure, and has told me not to mention it until Saturday. How can he expect me not to be excited? I have dreamed about this for so long.

I have booked a lovely hotel. It looks perfect from the brochure, and even has a lake and a gym. But what if Daniel doesn't like it?

Sunday 25 June

Weight 8st 11, alcohol units 7, cigarettes 2, calories 4587 (oh dear).

Oh dear. The weather has changed and suddenly it is freezing cold. I have brought only swimsuits, bikinis[55] and a long summer dress with me. I haven't brought anything for the cold weather.

There is a large wedding party at the hotel. Daniel and I are the only guests staying at the hotel who are not part of the wedding party.

5.30 p.m. Brrr. It's very cold. Daniel and I went down to the lake and took a rowing boat out on the water. But I didn't enjoy it because it was so cold. So we came back to our room for a hot bath.

As I came out of the bath, Daniel was lying on the bed laughing. 'I've got a new diet for you,' he said.

'So you *do* think I'm fat,' I replied.

'Don't be like that, Bridge,' he said. 'I keep telling you that men don't like thin women. They like women with large bottoms.'

I thought about this and wondered if Daniel was right.

'I'll just put the TV on,' Daniel said. He closed the curtains, so that the room was in darkness. After a few minutes, he began to watch the cricket. Then he lit a cigarette and called room service to order six cans of beer.

7

July: Huh

Sunday 2 July

Weight 8st 10, alcohol units 0, cigarettes 0, calories 995.

7.45 a.m. Mum just rang. 'Oh, hello, darling,' she said. 'Guess what?'

'I'll just go into the other room,' I said. I looked nervously over towards Daniel. Then I took the phone into the next room. My mother kept on talking.

'Hello? Oh, hello, darling, guess what?' she said again.

'What?' I asked.

'Una and Geoffrey are having a fancy dress[56] party in the garden on the twenty-ninth of July. Don't you think that's fun! Anyway, we thought it would be super if you and – ' she paused – 'Daniel, could come. We all want to meet him.'

'I don't think Daniel would really want to – ' I began.

'What's going on?' asked Daniel. He was standing naked in the doorway. 'Who are you talking to?'

'My mother,' I said, out of the corner of my mouth.

'Give it to me,' he said, taking the phone. 'Mrs Jones,' he said in his most charming voice. 'It's Daniel here. It's very early for a phone call on a Sunday morning. What can we do for you?'

He looked at me while she chatted for a few seconds, then he turned back to the phone.

'Well, that will be lovely. I shall put the date in my diary. Now, we'd better get back and get some sleep. Goodbye.' He turned to me. 'You see,' he said, 'you just have to be firm[57]. That's all.'

Saturday 22 July

Weight 8st 11 (must lose some), alcohol units 2, cigarettes 7, calories 1562.

I'm really excited about Daniel coming to the fancy dress party with me next Saturday. It will be a beautiful hot day. Maybe we could even have another minibreak and stay in a pub, or a hotel without televisions in the bedrooms.

I'm really looking forward to Daniel meeting my dad. I hope he likes him.

Friday 28 July

Weight 8st 12 (must go on a diet tomorrow), alcohol units 1, cigarettes 8, calories 345.

Mmmm. Daniel was really sweet tonight and helped me choose my costume for the party. I'm going to dress up as a 'Bunny Girl', with a tight black costume, stockings[58], two rabbit ears and a white bunny tail.

Sometimes I think Daniel cares about me a lot. Ooh, I'm so looking forward to tomorrow.

Saturday 29 July

Weight 8st 11, alcohol units 7, cigarettes 8, calories 6245.

2 p.m. I cannot believe what has happened. By 1 p.m. Daniel had still not woken up and I was starting to worry because the party starts at 2.30. At last I woke him with a cup of coffee.

'I thought you needed to wake up because we're supposed to be there at two-thirty,' I said.

'Where?' he asked.

'The fancy dress party.'

'Oh God, Bridget. Listen, I've got a lot of work to do this weekend. I'm really going to have to stay at home and do it.'

I couldn't believe it. He *promised* to come. Now nobody at the party will believe that I have a boyfriend.

10 p.m. I cannot believe what has happened to me today. I drove to the Alconburys' in my bunny girl costume and parked outside the house. I could hear voices coming from the garden. As I started to walk across the lawn, I realized that all the ladies were wearing normal skirts and dresses, and the men were wearing ordinary trousers and jumpers. Everybody was staring at me.

Then Una Alconbury came across the lawn.

'Bridget! It's lovely to see you. Come and have a drink.'

'I thought it was supposed to be a fancy dress party,' I said.

'Oh dear, didn't Geoffrey call you?' she said. 'We changed our minds. We're all looking forward to meeting your boyfriend,' she said, looking around. 'Where is he?'

'He had to work,' I said very quietly.

'How's my Bridget?' said Uncle Geoffrey. He was drunk.

'Why is your boyfriend working on a Saturday?' asked Una. 'That's not a very good excuse, is it? How are you going to get married like this?'

I could feel someone's eyes on me and looked up to see Mark Darcy. He was staring at my bunny tail. Beside him was Natasha, the tall thin girl who had been at the party for *Kafka's Motorbike*. She was wearing a pretty summer dress and had sunglasses on her head.

'Have you come from another party?' she asked, looking me up and down.

'Actually, I'm just on my way to work,' I said. Mark smiled and looked away.

'Hello, darling,' said my mother, hurrying towards us in a bright blue dress. 'What *are* you wearing, Bridget?' She went away towards Julio. I quickly looked around for Dad, but I couldn't see him.

Everybody was staring at me.

I saw Mark Darcy talking to Una and looking at me. Then Una came hurrying across.

'Bridget, I am *so* sorry about the mix-up over the fancy dress,' she said. 'Mark said you must be feeling very uncomfortable. Would you like to borrow a dress to wear?'

Una gave me a bridesmaid's[59] dress that had belonged to her daughter. I put it on over my bunny girl costume.

Later, Una was talking to me when Mark came up.

'What a pity Bridget couldn't bring her boyfriend,' she said. 'What's his name, Bridget? Daniel, is it? Your mother says he's one of these smart young publishers.'

'Daniel Cleaver?' asked Mark Darcy.

'Yes, it is, actually,' I said.

'Is he a friend of yours, Mark?' asked Una.

'Absolutely not,' said Mark.

'Oooh. I hope he's good enough for our Bridget,' said Una.

'I think I could say again, *absolutely not*,' said Mark.

But Una wasn't listening. She went away.

'I suppose you think it's OK to say bad things about my boyfriend to my parent's friends,' I said to Mark. 'You only did it because you're jealous.'

Mark stared at me with a shocked look on his face.

'Are you suggesting that I'm jealous of Daniel Cleaver?' he said. 'Because of you?'

'No, not because of me,' I said.

'Mark, darling,' said Natasha, coming across the lawn. 'Come and talk to your mother.'

'Just take care of yourself, that's all,' Mark said to me. 'And tell your mum to look after herself as well.' He looked over towards Mum and Julio.

I left the party shortly afterwards. I sat in my car for a few minutes, smoking a cigarette, before I felt calm enough to drive. When I got back to London, I decided to go round and see Daniel.

I rang the doorbell of Daniel's flat. There was no answer. I rang the doorbell again. Still no answer. Then I looked up at the window and saw Daniel's face. I smiled, waved at him and pointed to the door. His face disappeared. I waited. Then I rang the doorbell again.

At last Daniel's voice said on the entry phone system:

'Hi, Bridge. I'm just on the phone to America. Can I meet you in the pub in ten minutes?'

'OK,' I said happily and started walking towards the pub. When I reached the corner, I turned round. Daniel was at the window again, watching me.

Why was he watching me? Why hadn't he answered the door first time? Why didn't he let me come up straight away? Suddenly I knew the answer. He was with a woman. I went back to his flat and rang the doorbell again.

'Let me in,' I said when he answered.

'I told you, I'm on the phone.'

'Let me in, Daniel,' I said. 'Just open the door.'

At last Daniel let me in. I knew there was a woman in Daniel's house. I just *knew*. We stood looking at each other in the sitting-room.

'What have you got on?' asked Daniel.

'A bridesmaid's dress,' I said. I had forgotten I was wearing Una's daughter's dress.

'Would you like a drink?' asked Daniel.

'Yes, please,' I said. 'A cup of tea.'

Daniel went into the kitchen. As soon as he left the room, I started searching. I looked behind the sofa and in the cupboards.

'What are you doing?' said Daniel, coming back.

'Nothing,' I said quickly. 'I thought I might have left my skirt behind the sofa.'

Daniel went away. I went out of the living-room to the bathroom. I locked the door and searched that too. Then I went into Daniel's bedroom. Daniel was there, holding up a pair of jeans.

'Bridge,' he said. 'What are you doing in here?'

'I ... er ... came in here to look for you,' I said.

'I'll go and make the tea,' he said. He pushed me out of the bedroom and shut the door. I walked ahead of him back to the kitchen. Suddenly I saw the door which led up to the terrace on the roof. I opened the door, ran up the stairs and opened the door at the top.

There, spread out on a sunbed, was a golden, long-legged, naked woman. She raised her head, lifted her sunglasses and looked at me with one eye closed. I heard Daniel coming up the stairs behind me.

'Honey,' said the woman in an American accent, looking over my head at him. 'I thought you said she was *thin*.'

8

August: Depression

Tuesday 1 August

Weight 8st 12, alcohol units 3, cigarettes 40, calories 450 (I don't want to eat).

5 a.m. I'm very depressed. My boyfriend is sleeping with a golden woman with long legs. My mother is sleeping with a Portuguese man. I want to ring Daniel. But Tom has stuck a piece of paper to my telephone which says, *Do not ring Daniel or you will regret*[60] *it.*

I hate being alone in the middle of the night, smoking and crying. Oh God, what's wrong with me? Why does nothing ever work out? It's because I am too fat. Shall I ring Tom again? No. I only rang him forty-five minutes ago.

After I found the woman on the roof I didn't say anything to Daniel. I walked downstairs, got into my car and drove away. I went straight to Tom's. Tom gave me a large drink. When I got home, there were three messages from Daniel on my answerphone, asking me to call him. But I didn't.

Oh God, the birds have started singing. I have to go to work in three and a half hours. I can't do it. Help, help. I've had an idea. I'll ring Mum.

10 a.m. Mum was brilliant. 'Darling,' she said. 'Of course you haven't woken me. I'm just leaving for the TV studio. I can't believe you're acting this way over a stupid *man*. Forget about him. Go back to sleep. Go into work looking beautiful. Let everyone – including Daniel – see that you don't care about him. You'll be fine.'

'Oh, but Mum, I have to work with Daniel. I – '

'Darling, that's the wrong way round. He has to work with you. Anyway, it's time you got out of that job. I'm going to get you a job in television.'

I'm just going to work. I'm wearing a lot of make-up and a smart suit.

Thursday 3 August

Weight 8st 11, alcohol units 0, cigarettes 25.

Daniel kept sending me computer messages at work. 'We should talk.'

I didn't take any notice of them. But then tonight he came up to me outside the office as I was leaving. 'Darling, please, we really need to talk.'

I foolishly went for a drink with him. He kept saying, 'I feel so terrible. I really miss you.'

But when I said, 'Oh, Daniel, I miss you too,' he said, 'The thing is, Suki and I … '

'*Suki?*' I said. What a strange name.

'Oh, I can't explain. It's very special. I'm sorry, love,' he said, taking out his credit card and trying to get the attention of the waiter, 'but we're going to get married.'

Friday 4 August

Negative thoughts 600 every minute, crying attacks 12 (but only in the toilets).

Office. Third-floor toilets. Why did I think it was a good idea to have an affair with my boss?

I heard Daniel on the phone, talking to Suki and arranging to meet her tonight. He said, 'Not too bad … so far.' I knew he was talking about me.

Tuesday 8 August

9st, alcohol units 7, cigarettes 29, calories 5 million, negative thoughts 0, general thoughts 0.

I just called Jude. I told her about Daniel and she was very shocked. She said she would call Shazzer and arrange for us all to meet at nine.

Wednesday 9 August

Weight 9st 2, alcohol units 0 (but I had so many last night), cigarettes 0.

8 a.m. I'm very happy after the night out with Jude and Shazzer. We spent the evening talking about men and what emotional cowards they are.

9 a.m. Mum just rang. 'Darling,' she said. 'Guess what? *Good Afternoon!* are looking for researchers[61]. You know, that TV news and current affairs[62] programme. They're terribly good. I've spoken to Richard Finch, the editor, and told him all about you. He wants you to come in on Monday for a chat.'

Monday. Oh my God. That only gives me five days to learn about current affairs.

Saturday 12 August

Weight 9st 3, alcohol units 3 (very good), cigarettes 32 (very bad), calories 1800, number of articles about current affairs 1.5, minutes spent having imaginary conversations with Daniel 120 (very good).

Right. I am going to be very positive about everything. I am going to change my life. I am going to learn everything about current affairs and stop smoking completely. I am going to form a mature relationship with an adult man.

6.45 p.m. I was just starting to watch the 6 o'clock news, to learn about current affairs, when Mum came into my flat, carrying bags.

'Now, darling,' she said, 'I've brought you some smart suits of mine for Monday!'

I looked in the bags and saw something bright yellow.

'Er, Mum ... ' I began, but my mother's phone was ringing.

'Ah, that will be Julio,' she said, and started talking to him. 'Put the suit on,' she said to me.

Now she has gone off to a party, leaving me dressed in a bright blue suit with a green blouse and lots of blue eyeshadow.

'Don't be silly, darling,' she said. 'If you don't do *something* about your appearance, you'll never get a new job, never mind another boyfriend!'

Midnight. After she'd gone, I called Tom, who took me to a party. It was the party of a friend of his from art school. I met someone there called Gav. He was about twenty-two. But then I saw Daniel and I felt really upset again. I went into the toilets and started to cry.

Tom was waiting outside. 'Come and talk to Gav,' he said, 'He really likes you.' But then he looked at my face and said, 'Oh dear. I'll take you home.'

It's no good. When someone leaves you, you miss them very badly. And you feel that there's something wrong with you. They didn't want you. So you lose all your confidence.

Sunday 13 August

I couldn't sleep last night so I tried to read a magazine. There was a photo of Mark Darcy inside. It was in an article about London's fifty most eligible[63] bachelors – the fifty richest unmarried men in London.

Monday 14 August

I'm terrified about my interview with *Good Afternoon!* I've told Perpetua I have to go to the doctor's. Oh, the telephone is ringing.

I can't believe it. It was Richard Finch's personal assistant. She had a South London accent and sounded very young. Richard Finch is away in Blackpool this morning. So the interview has been changed to Wednesday.

Wednesday 16 August

I went to the interview. First I met Richard Finch's personal assistant, Patchouli. She was wearing cycle shorts and she had a nose ring.

Several men were sitting round a table. Most of them were very young. But one of them was middle-aged with curly blond hair. This was Richard Finch. He was talking to the young men excitedly. Suddenly, he looked at me.

'You must be Bridget!' he shouted. 'Tell me, why do you want a job in television?'

My mind went blank. I couldn't think what to say. I couldn't remember anything about politics or current affairs.

'Er … I have to leave my job because I slept with my boss,' I said.

There was a silence. Then Richard Finch started to laugh and all the young men started to laugh as well.

'Bridget Jones,' said Richard at last. 'Welcome to *Good Afternoon!* Take a seat, my darling.'

Monday 28 August

I got a letter from Richard Finch offering me a job, I think. This is all it said.

OK, my darling. You're on.

Tuesday 29 August

Weight 9st 2, alcohol units 0 (very good), cigarettes 3 (good), calories 1456.

10.30 a.m. Office. I just called Patchouli. She said I must start in a week. I don't know anything about television. But I don't want to work with Daniel any more. I had better go and tell him.

11.15 a.m. I can't believe this. Daniel stared at me, white-faced. 'You can't do this,' he said. 'Have you any idea how difficult the last few weeks have been for me?'

Then Perpetua burst in – she must have been listening outside the door.

'Daniel,' she shouted. 'How can you be so selfish? It was you who finished with Bridget. So let her go.'

I suddenly love Perpetua.

9

September: A New Job

Monday 4 September

Weight 9st, alcohol units 0, cigarettes 27, calories 15, minutes spent having imaginary conversations with Daniel 145 (good, better).

8 a.m. Today is the first day at my new job.

8.30 a.m. Mum just rang. I thought she was going to wish me good luck.

'Guess what, darling?' she began. 'Elaine and Malcolm have invited you to their ruby wedding[64] party! They've been married for forty years and they're having a party to celebrate.'

Who were Elaine and Malcolm? Oh, yes – Mark Darcy's parents.

'He told Elaine he thought you were very attractive,' my mother said.

'Really?' I said, feeling pleased.

'Well, I'm sure that's what he meant, anyway, darling.'

'What exactly did he say?' I asked.

'He said you were very ... well, "bizarre".'

'But, Mother ... "bizarre" means "weird",' I said.

'Yes, but it's a lovely word, isn't it,' said my mother. 'Anyway, you can ask him all about it at the wedding party.'

9 p.m. I'm in bed, completely exhausted. Starting a new job is very tiring.

There was a meeting at 9.30. I was late, but it wasn't my fault. I was stopped at the door of the TV studios by the security guards.

I had to wait until Patchouli, Richard's assistant, came to get me. She arrived at last with two huge dogs.

'They're Richard's,' she said, dragging the dogs away. 'Aren't they brilliant! I'll just take them out to the car.'

'Won't I be late for the meeting?' I asked, but Patchouli wasn't listening.

So by the time I got into the office, the meeting had started. Everyone turned round and stared at me. It was really embarrassing.

Saturday 9 September

Weight 8st 12, alcohol units 4, cigarettes 10, calories 1876, minutes spent having imaginary conversations with Daniel 24 (excellent).

11.30 a.m. I was just preparing my breakfast when suddenly my mother burst into my flat.

'Guess what, darling?' she said.

'What?' I asked.

'Malcolm and Elaine are having the ruby wedding party at Mark's house. Mark's bought a big house in Holland Park, that very fashionable area ... What are you going to wear?'

'Are you going with Julio or Dad?' I asked.

'Oh, darling, I don't know. Probably both of them,' she said.

'You can't do that.'

'But Daddy and I are still friends, darling. I'm just friends with Julio as well. Anyway, I'll tell Elaine you'd love to come, shall I? I must go. Bye!'

Saturday 23 September

Weight 9st, alcohol units 0, cigarettes O, replies written to Mark Darcy's invitation 14 (but writing the replies has replaced the imaginary conversations with Daniel).

10 a.m. Right. I am going to reply to Mark Darcy's invitation and tell him I won't be able to go to his party. There is no reason for me to go. Anyway, I would miss my favourite TV programmes.

Oh! The telephone is ringing.

It was Dad. 'Bridget, are you coming to the Darcys' party next Saturday?' he said. 'Your mother and that Portuguese man will be there. I want to show them I don't care and I need you to support me. Please come.'

11.30 a.m. I've replied to Mark Darcy. I've accepted his invitation.

Tuesday 26 September

Weight 8st 13, alcohol units 0, cigarettes 0, calories 1256, thoughts about Daniel 0, negative thoughts 0.

I'm getting on really well at *Good Afternoon!* I think I might have a special talent for popular TV programmes.

Richard Finch has got an idea about fire stations. He wants me to go to a fire station in Lewisham in South London and interview the firemen. I have to go there tomorrow at 11 a.m.

I am going to be on television. I am going to ring all my friends and tell them to watch the programme. I'm going to tell Mum straightaway.

Wednesday 27 September

Weight 8st 11 (I've lost weight because I'm so embarrassed), alcohol units 3, cigarettes 0 (I wasn't allowed to smoke in the fire station) but then I had 12 within an hour, calories 1584.

9 p.m. I've never been so embarrassed in my life. I spent all day getting ready for the interviews at the fire station.

Richard Finch had told me that, when they started filming at five o'clock, I had to slide down the fireman's pole[65]. The firemen use this pole when they are called out to an emergency.

At five o'clock I was ready at the top of the pole. Suddenly I heard Richard's voice in my earpiece shouting, 'Go, go, go, go, go!' so I started to slide down the pole. Then he shouted again, 'Newcastle, go, go, go! Bridget, wait in Lewisham. We'll film you in about thirty seconds.'

But it was too late. I was halfway down the pole. I started to try and pull myself back up. Then suddenly Richard shouted again.

'Bridget! What are you doing? The camera's on you now. You're supposed to be sliding down the pole, not trying to climb up it. Go, go, go.'

I smiled in a mad kind of way at the camera and dropped myself down. I landed at the feet of the fireman I was supposed to interview.

'Lewisham, we've run out of time,' shouted Richard in my ear. 'Finish the interview, Bridget.'

'And now – back to the studio!' I said.

Thursday 28 September

Weight 8st 12, alcohol units 2, cigarettes 11, calories 1850, job offers from fire stations and other TV stations 0 (not really surprising).

11 a.m. Everyone is laughing at me. Everyone is saying, 'And now – back to the studio!' They all think it's very funny.

Patchouli came up to me.

'That fireman's pole idea was really brilliant,' she said. 'Now – back to the studio!'

I'm so depressed. I thought I'd found something I was good at, but I'm no good at anything. Not men. Not social skills. Not work. Nothing.

But it was too late. I was halfway down the pole.

10

October: A Date with Darcy

Weight 8st 11, alcohol units 0 (very good, especially for a party).

4 a.m. I've had a very surprising evening.

Dad and I went to the Darcys' ruby wedding party. I had a shock when we arrived. Mark Darcy's house is huge. It is painted white and looks like a wedding cake. All the trees around were hung with red lights and shiny red hearts, to celebrate the ruby wedding.

We went down a stairway lit by heart-shaped candles on each step. The stairs led down into a huge room leading on to the garden. The whole room was lit by candles. The waiters brought round large silver trays with champagne and delicious food. All the guests were happy and laughing.

The only guests who were not happy were my mother and Una Alconbury.

'What do you think of this party, Pam?' Una said to my mother.

'I think it's very showy[66],' said my mother. 'The Darcys just want everyone to know how much money they have.'

I glanced round nervously. There, very near us, was Mark Darcy. He must have heard everything. I started to say something, but he walked away.

It was time for dinner. The guests stood in a line, waiting to be shown to their seats. Mark Darcy was standing just in front of me.

'Hi,' I said. I was sorry about my mother's rudeness and I wanted to make the situation better. Mark looked round, but then he looked away.

'Hi,' I said in a louder voice. He turned round again.

'Oh, hi, I'm sorry. I didn't see you,' he said.

'It's a great party,' I said. 'Thanks for inviting me.'

Mark stared at me for a moment. 'Oh, I didn't invite you,' he said. 'My mother invited you.' He turned round and went away. Then Natasha appeared, wearing a beautiful gold dress, and took his arm.

All the guests had places at the table with their names on cards. I was sitting next to Geoffrey Alconbury. 'So how's my little Bridget?' said Uncle Geoffrey. 'Una tells me you've broken up with your boyfriend. When are we going to get you married off?'

After the meal, I decided to go and look at Elaine and Malcolm's ruby wedding presents. I went into the room where the presents were on show.

'What are you doing?' said a voice. It was Mark.

I didn't know what to say. Perhaps he thought I was trying to steal the presents.

'I'm just looking at the presents,' I said.

Just then Natasha appeared in the doorway. 'Oh, hi,' she said when she saw me. 'Aren't you wearing your bunny girl costume today?' She laughed.

I went outside for some fresh air and a cigarette. It was a wonderful, warm night. The moon and stars shone brightly.

A young boy approached me. He was blond and quite attractive.

'Hi,' said the boy. He lit a cigarette and came towards me. 'I'm Simon. Would you like to dance? I mean, out here in the garden. Just for a moment.'

'I don't know,' I said.

'Please,' said Simon. 'I've never danced with an older woman before. Oh, sorry, I didn't mean …' He took my hand and we started dancing. Then a voice said,

'That's enough now, Simon.' It was Mark Darcy. 'Go back inside.'

Simon walked off in an embarrassed way.

'Bridget, will you dance with me?' asked Mark.

'No,' I said. Then I went on, 'But I'm very glad you asked me to your party. It's fantastic. Thank you very much.'

Mark started walking around. He pushed his hands through his hair.

'Bridget,' he said. 'I … have you read any good books lately?'

I couldn't believe it. Mark Darcy was asking me about books again. It was the same question that he had asked me at Una Alconbury's Turkey Lunch.

'Mark,' I said. 'Why don't you ask me something else?'

'Well,' he said, 'I … will you have dinner with me, Bridget?'

I stopped and stared at him suspiciously.

'Did my mum tell you to ask me that?' I said. 'Or Una Alconbury?'

'No,' he replied.

'Please don't ask me if I've read any good books again,' I said.

He stared at me. 'But Una Alconbury told me you know a lot about books,' he explained. 'And that you have a very glamorous[67] life with millions of men taking you out. I heard about Daniel. I'm sorry.'

'Why don't you like him?' I asked.

'He slept with my wife,' replied Mark. 'It was two weeks after our wedding.'

I stared at him in shock. Then a voice shouted from the house,

'Mark!' It was Natasha. 'Mark! What are you doing down there?'

'You're so different from all the other girls I know,' said Mark. 'No other girl would wear a bunny tail or …'

'Mark!' shouted Natasha again.

'But you're going out with Natasha,' I said.

'I'm not any more,' he said. 'Let's have dinner sometime, all right?'

'OK,' I whispered. 'OK.'

I gave Mark my address and phone number, and we arranged to have dinner next Tuesday.

Tuesday 3 October

Weight 8st 12, alcohol units 3 (very good), cigarettes 21 (bad).

7.30 p.m. I'm in a complete panic. Mark Darcy is coming round to pick me up in half an hour. I've just got home from work and I need to wash my hair.

7.50 p.m. Oh God, oh God. I still haven't washed my hair. I'll quickly get into the bath.

8.00 p.m. I'm drying my hair now with my hairdryer. I very much hope Mark Darcy is late because I'm still not ready.

8.05 p.m. My hair is almost dry now. I just have to put on my make-up.

8.15 p.m. He's still not here.

8.20 p.m. I'm almost ready now. Perhaps I'll change my dress.

8.30 p.m. This is weird. He's more than half an hour late.

9.00 p.m. I can't believe it. Mark Darcy has decided not to come. The rat!

Thursday 5 October

Weight 8st 13 (bad), chocolate bars 4.

11 a.m. I'm in the toilets at work. Richard Finch has given me a job to do.

'Right, Bridget,' he said. 'It's the end of the Isabella Rossellini trial[68] today. They're going to decide if she's innocent or guilty. Go down to the High Court[69] and interview her.'

I had no idea what he was talking about.

'You do know who Isabella Rossellini is, don't you?' said Richard. 'You do read the newspapers sometimes?'

'Yes, of course,' I said. I didn't want to say that I had never heard of Isabella Rossellini.

I'm going to meet the camera crew at the law courts. I have to report on a story for television without knowing what it is about.

11.05 a.m. I just came out of the toilets and found Patchouli outside with Richard's dogs.

'Are you OK?' she asked. 'You look a bit worried.'

'No, no, I'm fine,' I said.

'Are you sure?' She stared at me for a moment. 'Listen, Richard didn't mean Isabella Rossellini. He's thinking of Elena Rossini, right?'

Oh, now I understand! Elena Rossini is a children's nanny[70]. She's accused of murdering her employer. But she says she killed him because he tried to attack her.

I grabbed a couple of newspapers and ran for a taxi.

3 p.m. I can't believe what just happened. I was outside the High Court with a crowd of reporters. We were waiting for the trial to end when I realized I needed some cigarettes.

'Do you think it's OK if I go to the shop on the corner?' I asked the cameraman.

'Yes,' he said. 'I'll come and get you if the trial ends and Elena comes out.'

I was just standing in the shop when a man came in.

'Can you give me a box of chocolates?' he asked.

I turned round. It was Mark Darcy. He was wearing the clothes lawyers wear in court. He just stared at me.

'Where were you last night?' I asked.

'I'd like to ask you the same question,' he replied coldly.

Then the camera assistant rushed into the shop. 'Bridget!' he shouted. 'We've missed the interview. Elena Rossini's come out and gone.'

'Missed the interview?' I said. 'Oh God. I'll be sacked – I'll lose my job. Did the other reporters get interviews with her?'

'Actually, nobody got interviews,' said Mark Darcy.

'Didn't they?' I said. 'But how do you know?'

'Because I was the lawyer who was defending[71] her, and I told her not to give any interviews,' he said. 'Look, she's out there in my car.'

As I looked, Elena Rossini put her head out of the car window and shouted, 'Hurry up with my chocolates, Mark!'

'So where were you last night?' asked Mark Darcy.

'Waiting for you,' I said.

'What, at five past eight? I rang on your doorbell twelve times.'

'Yes, I was … drying my hair.'

'Do you have a big noisy hairdryer?' asked Mark suddenly.

'Yes,' I said proudly. 'Why?'

'Maybe you should get a quieter hairdryer or dry your hair earlier,' he said, laughing. 'Come on, get your cameraman. I'll see what I can do for you.'

Oh God. How embarrassing. I feel like such an idiot.

9 p.m. I'm so happy! Thanks to Mark, I was the only reporter to get an interview with Elena Rossini. My interview was broadcast on the *Good Afternoon!* programme today. I recorded it and I've watched it five times.

I recorded it and I've watched it five times.

Friday 6 October

Weight 9 st, alcohol units 6, number of times I have checked to see if Mark Darcy has called 21, number of times I have watched video 9.

9 p.m. Mum rang tonight to talk about the Darcys' ruby wedding party. She kept saying how marvellous Mark Darcy was.

I keep hoping Mark might ring me up and ask me for another date after what happened with the hairdryer. Maybe I should write him a note to say thank you for the interview and sorry about the hairdryer.

Friday 13 October

Weight 9st 3, alcohol units 0, calories 0.

Oh, God, I'm so lonely. There's a whole weekend in front of me with no one to have fun with. But I don't care. I've got some nice food in my fridge.

11

November: A Criminal in the Family

Wednesday 1 November

Weight 8st 13, alcohol units 2 (very good), cigarettes 4.

Mark Darcy still hasn't called me. But Jude has had a brilliant idea.

'Why don't you have a dinner party and invite him?' she said. 'It's not like asking him on a date. All your friends will be there.'

Friday 3 November

Weight 9st 2, alcohol units 2, cigarettes 8, calories 5245.

11 a.m. I'm very excited about the idea of a dinner party. I've bought a marvellous new cookery book by a famous international chef. He makes cooking sound very easy.

Thursday 9 November

Weight 8st 13, alcohol units 5, cigarettes 12, calories 1456.

I've decided to have the dinner party on Tuesday 21 November. Mark Darcy seemed very pleased when I rang him up.

'What are you going to cook?' he said. 'Are you good at cooking?'

'Actually, I'm going to use a recipé by a famous international chef,' I said.

Mark Darcy laughed. 'Well, don't do anything too complicated,' he said. 'Remember, everyone's coming to see *you*, not just to eat your food.'

Monday 20 November

Weight 8st 12 (very good), cigarettes 0, alcohol units 3, calories 200.

7 p.m. I've just got back from the supermarket. I bought a lot of things for the dinner party. I've got to start preparing the food tonight.

First, I'm going to make soup. The recipé says I have to boil some vegetables. I have to tie the vegetables together with string to make the soup taste better. But I only have bright blue string. Oh well, I'm sure it will be OK.

I'm going to make a lovely dessert with oranges. I bought thirty-six oranges from the supermarket. Now I have to peel them and slice them. It won't take long.

1 a.m. I'm too tired to stay awake now.

Tuesday 21 November

Weight 8st 11, alcohol units 9 (very bad), cigarettes 37 (very very bad), calories 3479 (terrible).

5 p.m. Oh God. This has been a terrible day. My mother rang me at work.

'Hello, darling, it's Mummy here. I just called to say goodbye before I go.'

'Go? Go where?' I asked.

'Oh. Julio and I are going to Portugal for a couple of weeks,' she replied. 'Er Bridget … I was just wondering … Could you lend me some money? Just a couple of hundred pounds.'

'I'm in the middle of work,' I said. 'How will I get the money to you?'

'I'm outside the bank just across the road from your office,' she said. 'Meet me there in five minutes.'

I went downstairs to the cashpoint machine and took some money out. Just then, I saw my mother hurrying towards me. It was raining but she was wearing sunglasses.

'Oh, there you are, darling. You are sweet,' she said, grabbing the money from my hand. 'Thank you very much. I must go. Goodbye!'

'What's going on?' I asked suspiciously. 'What are you doing here? Why can't Julio lend you the money?'

For a moment she looked frightened, then she smiled.

'I'll be fine,' she said. 'Take care.' She hugged me quickly then she ran back across the road.

7 p.m. I just got home. Right. I must keep calm. I'll put the soup in the pan with the vegetables tied with string.

8.30 p.m. Everything is going very well. The guests are all in the living room. Mark Darcy brought champagne and a box of chocolates.

8.35 p.m. Oh my God. I just looked in the pan. The dye[72] has come off the string and coloured the soup. Now the soup is bright blue.

9 p.m. I love my friends. They didn't mind about the blue soup. Mark Darcy said that there is nothing wrong with blue food.

9.30 p.m. Mark Darcy and Jude came into the kitchen and helped me make a big omelette with eggs, and fried potatoes. At least the orange dessert will be good.

10 p.m. I am very disappointed. The orange dessert tasted like marmalade[73]. I have failed at cooking. After all the time and money I've spent on this meal, I have served my friends with:

Blue soup
Omelette
Marmalade

I didn't think things could get any worse. But after the meal was cleared away, the phone rang. It was Dad.

'I'm sorry, Bridget. I'm afraid there's been some rather bad news.'

'What?' I asked.

'Your mother and Julio are wanted by the police.'

2 a.m. I'm in a single bed in Una and Geoffrey Alconbury's spare room.

When Dad told me the news about Mum and Julio, I was very shocked.

'What's happened?' I asked.

'I'm afraid they have stolen money from a large number of people,' Dad explained, 'including myself and some of our closest friends. Your mother may have to go to prison.'

'Oh my God. What did they do?'

'Julio pretended that he owned some time-share[74] apartments in Portugal. Your mother persuaded our friends to buy the apartments. They gave Julio money. People like Una and Geoffrey, and Malcolm and Elaine Darcy.'

Oh my God. Mark Darcy's parents.

'So what happened?'

'The apartments didn't exist. Your mother gave Julio a lot of money too. She has borrowed money from the bank and re-mortgaged[75] our house. So if we can't pay the money back to the bank, they can take our house away. We'll have no home, and your mother will be a criminal.'

Jude came into the room. I told her what had happened. She didn't say anything, but immediately went to fetch Mark Darcy.

'This is all my fault,' he said. 'I knew there was something wrong about Julio. I heard him talking on the phone at the fancy dress party. But I didn't know he had taken money from my parents. Where's your mother now?'

'I don't know,' I said. 'Portugal, I think.'

'Where's your father?' asked Mark. 'Would you like to go to him?'

'He's at Una and Geoffrey Alconbury's place,' I said.

Mark and I drove up to the Alconburys' house. Several of our friends were also there. They were eating sandwiches and drinking wine and discussing what to do. Mark walked around, making phone calls. It was terrible, but it was also rather exciting.

Wednesday 22 November

Weight 8st 10, alchohol units 3, cigarettes 27, calories 5671.

10 a.m. I'm back in my flat. I didn't get any sleep last night and now I've got to go to work. Richard Finch will be angry because I'm late.

Mark Darcy went back to London very early in the morning. I left a message on his answer-phone saying thank you for helping.

Una and Geoffrey told me not to worry about Dad because they will look after him.

Saturday 25 November

Weight 9st, alcohol units 2, cigarettes 3, calories 4567.

Thank God. Dad has had a phone call from Mum. She said not to worry and that she was safe. The police checked the line, and found out that she was calling from Portugal.

I am going to see Dad this afternoon. I wish Mark Darcy would ring.

1 p.m. Just as I was leaving, Mark Darcy called. He was ringing from Portugal. He said the police there have found Mum. Mark thinks she won't have to go to prison because she didn't know what Julio was doing. The police haven't found Julio yet.

Mum is coming back tonight, but she will have to go straight to a police station for questioning.

Sunday 26 November

Weight 9st 1, alcohol units 0, cigarettes 1, calories 188.

It's been a terrible day. Dad and I went to the airport to meet Mum this evening. Two policemen were with her.

Dad and I thought that Mum would feel ashamed[76] because of what had happened. But she wasn't ashamed at all.

'Let me go,' she kept saying to the policemen. 'I'm back in Britain now. I don't want everyone to see me with the police.'

'You have to go with them, Mum,' I said. 'You have to find out if they are going to arrest you.'

At last Mum got into the back of the police car and it drove away.

Monday 27 November

Weight 9st 1, alcohol units 0, cigarettes 50, hours of sleep 0.

9 a.m. I'm completely exhausted. Dad and I waited at the police station last night for two hours. At last we heard Mum's voice coming along a corridor.

'Yes, that's right. It's me. I'm on *Suddenly Single* every morning. Would you like me to sign my name for you?' She came round the corner. There was a policeman with her and she was wearing his helmet[77].

'Aren't they going to arrest you?' I asked.

'Don't be silly, darling,' she said, looking at the policeman, who turned red. 'Of course they're not going to arrest me.'

'So what happened?' I asked her when we were in the car.

Dad and I went to the airport to meet Mum this evening.
Two policemen were with her.

'Oh, it was just a silly problem,' said Mum. 'The Portuguese authorities[78] wouldn't give us planning permission[79] to build the apartments. But we had a super holiday!'

'Where is Julio?' I asked suspiciously.

'Oh, he's stayed behind in Portugal.'

We went back to Una and Geoffrey Alconbury's. Everyone looked angrily at Mum. So she decided to go straight to bed. Then the phone rang for Dad.

'That was Mark Darcy,' said Dad. 'He's still in Portugal. He's made a deal with Julio and he's got some of the money back.'

Everyone was very happy, and very grateful to Mark Darcy.

12

December: An Excellent Year's Progress

Monday 4 December

Weight 9st 2 (must lose some weight before Christmas), alcohol units 3, cigarettes 7, calories 3876 (oh dear).

I've just been to the supermarket. The shops are all beginning to get ready for Christmas.

Mark Darcy still hasn't called me.

Tuesday 5 December

Weight 9st 2 (I really am going to go on a diet today), alcohol units 4, cigarettes 10, calories 3245 (better).

Mark Darcy still hasn't called. Maybe he is too good to go out with me. I should go out with someone else – for example, Daniel.

I just called Shazzer. She said I must not go out with Daniel again.

2 a.m. Why hasn't Mark Darcy called me? Why? Why?

Friday 8 December

Weight 9st 5, alcohol units 4 (good), cigarettes 12 (excellent), Christmas presents bought 0, cards sent 0.

4 p.m. Humph. Jude just called. She said, 'See you at Rebecca's place on Sunday.'

'Rebecca's place?' I said. 'What's happening at Rebecca's?'

'Oh, hasn't she … ? She's just having a few friends round … I think it's a kind of dinner party.'

'I'm busy on Sunday,' I said. This wasn't true. But I didn't want to tell Jude that I hadn't been invited. Why had Rebecca invited Jude and not me?

9 p.m. I had a drink with Shazzer, and she said, 'What are you wearing to Rebecca's party on Sunday?'

Midnight. I must not get upset about not being invited to Rebecca's party. It's not important.

5.30 a.m. Why hasn't Rebecca invited me to her party? Why?

Saturday 9 December

Christmas parties to look forward to = 0.

7.45 a.m. I was woken up by a call from my mother.

'Hello, darling. Are you coming to the Vibrant TV party on Tuesday?' she asked brightly. '*Everyone's* going.'

Vibrant TV is the name of the TV company I work for.

'I haven't been invited,' I said.

'Maybe you haven't worked there long enough,' she said.

'But, Mum,' I interrupted, '*you* don't work for Vibrant TV.'

'Well, that's different, darling,' she said. 'I've got to go now. 'Bye!'

11.30 a.m. I called Tom to see if he wanted to go out tonight.

'Sorry,' he said. 'I'm busy. But I'll see you tomorrow at Rebecca's party.'

Tom has only met Rebecca twice and I've known her for nine years. So why has she invited Tom and not me?

2 p.m. I went shopping and bumped into Rebecca in a department store.

'Hi,' I said excitedly.

'Oh, hello,' she said in a cold voice. 'I can't stop to talk. I'm in a hurry.'

As she left the shop, I tried not to cry. Christmas is supposed to be a time of happiness – for families, romance, warmth and presents. But if you have no boyfriend, your mother is going out with a Portuguese criminal and your friends don't want you any more, it's very sad and lonely.

Monday 11 December

I returned from work to find a message from Rebecca on my answer-phone.

'Bridget. This is Rebecca. I know you work in TV now and you go to glamorous parties every night. I know you're too busy to come to an old friend's party. But you could have replied to my invitation.'

I called Rebecca immediately but there was no reply. I decided to go round to her place. As I was going downstairs, I met Dan, the Australian guy who lives in the flat underneath.

'Hi,' he said. 'Did you get your mail? I've been putting it under your door, so you don't have to come downstairs in the cold every morning.'

I rushed back upstairs and went into my flat. I lifted up the doormat. There, under the mat, was a little pile of letters, Christmas cards and invitations. They were all addressed to me!

Thursday 14 December

Weight 9st 3, alcohol units 2, cigarettes 14, calories 1500.

Parties, parties, parties! Everyone is inviting me to Christmas parties.

Friday 22 December

It's nearly Christmas. I've started thinking about Daniel again. I can't believe that he hasn't sent me a Christmas card.

Saturday 23 December

Weight 9st 4, alcohol units 12, cigarettes 38, calories 2976.

6.45 p.m. Oh God, I'm so lonely. Even Jude has forgotten about me. She's with Vile Richard tonight.

7.p.m. Jude called me. She was crying. Jude is coming round. She'll be here by 7.30. Vile Richard has gone back to his old girlfriend.

8 p.m. Daniel just called. He was very drunk. 'I ... love you, Jones,' he said. 'I've made a terrible mistake ... Stupid Suki made of plastic ... I'm coming round.'

Midnight. Humph. Neither of them came round. Vile Richard changed his mind and came back to Jude. And Daniel called at 10 o'clock. He said he was watching the football.

Huh. I'm completely alone. My whole year has been a failure.

Sunday 24 December

Weight 9st 4, alcohol units 1, cigarettes 2, calories 1 million, number of warm festive thoughts = 0.

Midnight. I'm at my parents' house. Once again, I am spending Christmas Eve alone in my parents' house in a single bed. It's so embarrassing.

Monday 25 December

Weight 9st 5, alcohol units 2, cigarettes 3, calories 2657, number of crazy Christmas presents = 12.

12.30 p.m. I went downstairs to find Mum and Una in the kitchen, preparing the vegetables for Christmas dinner. Every Christmas my mother and Una have a terrible argument about the gravy, the sauce made with the juices from the turkey. Both of them think they know the best way to make gravy.

They had just started arguing when there was a terrible crash. Then a figure burst through the French windows[80] from the garden. It was Julio. He was holding a bottle of wine. He walked over to my Dad.

'You sleep with my woman,' he said.

'Ah,' said Dad. 'Merry Christmas, er … Would you like a drink?'

'You sleep,' said Julio dangerously, 'with my woman.' He looked very wild, drunk and exciting.

'Oh, Julio, you naughty person,' said Mum in a voice like a little girl. Oh God. She was still in love with Julio.

'You sleep,' said Julio, pointing at Dad, 'with him.' Then he rushed upstairs.

'Please can you ask everyone to sit down,' said Mum to Dad. 'And start serving dinner.' She followed Julio upstairs.

I looked out of the window and had a great shock. Mark Darcy was walking across the garden. The next minute he had entered the living-room through the French windows.

'Everyone keep quiet,' he said. 'The police are outside. I'm not sure if Julio's violent. We need to get your mum to come downstairs. Then the police can go upstairs and arrest him.'

I had a brilliant idea. I knew exactly how to get Mum to come down.

'OK. Leave it to me,' I said. I walked to the bottom of the stairs.

'You sleep,' said Julio, pointing at Dad, 'with him.'

'Mum!' I shouted. 'Una is spoiling the gravy! Can you come down?'

Immediately my mother ran downstairs and into the kitchen. Two policemen ran upstairs and brought down Julio. They took him away.

Suddenly I felt a strong hand on my arm.

'Come on,' said Mark Darcy.

'What?' I said.

'Don't say "what", Bridget, say "pardon",' said Mum.

'Mrs Jones,' said Mark firmly. 'I am taking Bridget away to celebrate Christmas.'

I took Mark Darcy's hand.

'Merry Christmas, everyone,' I said. 'I expect we'll see you all at the New Year's Day Turkey Lunch.'

This is what happened next.

Mark Darcy took me to a hotel for champagne and Christmas lunch. It was very easy to talk to him. He told me all about Julio. Mark had met Julio in Portugal. But Julio had refused to return the money he'd stolen.

'But then I thought of a way to make Julio come back to England,' Mark said.

'What?'

'Don't say "what", Bridget, say "pardon",' he said, and I laughed. 'I realised that Julio really loves your mother,' Mark went on. 'So I told him she was spending Christmas with your Dad. Julio was so jealous that he came straight back to England. So then the police could arrest him.'

'That was very kind of you,' I said. 'But why did you do it?'

'Bridget,' he said. 'Isn't it obvious?'

Oh God. I realised that everything Mark Darcy had done to help my family was because he loved me! It was a wonderful feeling.

Later we went upstairs and had more champagne.

'Why didn't you ring me up before Christmas?' I asked suspiciously. 'I left you *two* messages.'

'I didn't want to talk to you till I'd finished the job. And I didn't think you liked me very much.'

'*What?*'

'Don't you mean *pardon*?' he said, laughing.

January – December: A summary

Alcohol units 3836 (not good)
Cigarettes 5277
Weight gained 5st 2 lb
Weight lost 5st 3lb (excellent)
Valentines 1
Boyfriends 2
Nice boyfriends 1
Number of New Year Resolutions kept 1
An excellent year's progress!

Points for Understanding

1

1 Read Bridget's New Year's Resolutions. What can you learn from them about her?
2 Who is Mark Darcy? Why doesn't Bridget want to meet him?
3 Who are these people?
(a) Una Alconbury (b) Perpetua (c) Daniel Cleaver (d) Shazzer (e) Tom
4 Why does Bridget tell Daniel he is an emotional coward?

2

1 Why does Bridget call her married friends the 'Smug Marrieds'? What do they say to make her feel bad?
2 'Valentine's Day has no meaning.' How does Bridget really feel about Valentine's Day?
3 Why does Bridget's mother want to change her life? Why does Bridget not believe her mother is telling her the whole truth?

3

1 What advice do (a) Shazzer (b) Jude (c) Tom give about Daniel? Whose advice works best?
2 What problems does Bridget face in planning for her birthday?
3 'I love my friends.' Why does Bridget say this?
4 Name two ways in which Bridget's mother surprises her.

4

1 Why does Bridget want to develop 'inner poise'?
2 Why is Bridget surprised to see Jeremy in the restaurant? What problems does this cause for her?
3 How does Bridget feel about the book party? Read through her list of aims for the party. How successful is she in achieving them?
4 What information does Daniel give Bridget about Mark Darcy?

5

1 How does Bridget feel about being pregnant?
2 Who helps Bridget about the pregnancy test? What mistake has she made about the test?
3 What does Magda say about marriage that Bridget finds surprising?
4 Why is Bridget angry with her mother?

6

1 Where does Bridget want to go with Daniel?
2 What does Daniel like doing at weekends?
3 Why does Daniel not behave thoughtfully towards Bridget?

7

1 How does Daniel let Bridget down about the fancy dress party?
2 Why is Bridget embarrassed at the party? Whose fault is this?
3 Who is with Mark Darcy at the party? How does he behave thoughtfully towards Bridget?
4 What does Bridget suspect about Daniel? How does she find out the truth?

8

1 How does Bridget's mother help her?
2 Who are these people?
(a) Gav (b) Richard Finch (c) Patchouli
3 Why does Richard Finch offer Bridget a job at *Good Afternoon!*?

9

1 Why is Bridget late for the meeting?
2 Why does Bridget change her mind about going to Mark Darcy's party?
3 What happens to Bridget at the fire station?

10

1 How does Bridget's mother embarrass her at the Darcys' party?
2 Why does Mark come into the garden? What does he ask Bridget?
3 How do these cause things to go wrong for Bridget?
(a) a hairdryer (b) a shop selling cigarettes and sweets
4 Why is Bridget the only reporter to get an interview with Elena Rossini?

11

1 Why does Bridget decide to have a dinner party? What is she going to cook?
2 How do things go wrong with the food at the dinner party?
3 What news does Bridget's father have?
4 How does Mark Darcy show that he cares about Bridget?

12

1 Why is Bridget upset about Rebecca's party? Why is Rebecca upset with Bridget? What has happened to cause this?
2 Who comes unexpectedly to the Alconburys' place on Christmas Day?
3 How does Bridget get her mother to come downstairs?
4 How did Mark Darcy persuade Julio to come back to England?

Glossary

1 ***identified*** – *to identify with someone* (page 4)
to feel that you can understand and share someone else's feelings.

2 ***heroine*** (page 4)
the main female character of a book, film, or play, or a good female character.

3 ***affair*** (page 6)
a sexual relationship between two people, especially when one of them is married to someone else.

4 ***divorced*** (page 7)
no longer married because the marriage has been legally ended.

5 ***New Year's resolution*** (page 11)
a decision that you make on the first day of the year about the things that you intend to do or stop doing during that year.

6 ***mature*** (page 11)
a *mature* relationship is conducted in a sensible way that you would expect from adults, for example showing the knowledge and experience of how to deal with particular situations.

7 ***hug*** (page 12)
the action of putting your arms round someone to show your love or friendship.

8 ***eagerly*** (page 12)
in a way that shows you are interested or excited about something.

9 ***face*** – *to face something* (page 14)
to accept that a bad situation exists and try to deal with it.

10 ***bottom*** (page 14)
the part of your body that you sit on.

11 ***opinion*** (page 15)
the attitude that you have towards something, especially your thoughts about how good it is. If you have a *high opinion* of something or someone, you think that they are very good.

12 ***dare*** – *how dare he?* (page 15)
used for saying how shocked and angry you are about something that someone has done or said.

13 ***flash up*** (page 15)
to appear for a very short time and then quickly disappear.

14 ***absent*** (page 16)
not in the place where you should be or are expected to be.

15 ***marvellous*** (page 17)
extremely good.
16 ***point*** (page 17)
the reason for something. If someone says *what's the point?*, they are asking why they are doing something.
17 ***human rights*** (page 17)
the rights that everyone should have in a society, including the right to express opinions about the government or to have protection from harm.
18 ***exhausted*** (page 19)
extremely tired and without enough energy to do anything else.
19 ***harvesting*** (page 19)
the action of collecting a crop from the fields.
20 ***humph*** (page 19)
used for showing that you are annoyed or do not approve of something.
21 ***coward*** (page 20)
someone who is not brave enough to fight or do something difficult or dangerous that they should do.
22 ***Valentine's Day*** (page 21)
14 February, the day on which people give cards and small presents to the person who they love.
23 ***cool*** (page 21)
impressive because of being fashionable or attractive.
24 ***smug*** (page 21)
too satisfied with your abilities or achievements. This word shows that you dislike people like this.
25 ***decent*** (page 23)
good or good enough.
26 ***burst into*** (page 23)
if you *burst into* something, for example tears or laughter, you suddenly start doing something. Bridget suddenly starts to cry.
27 ***vanish*** (page 23)
to disappear in a sudden and mysterious way.
28 ***cool*** (page 23)
not friendly or enthusiastic.
29 ***grin*** (page 24)
a big smile that shows your teeth.
30 ***weird*** (page 24)
strange and unusual, sometimes in a way that upsets you.

31 ***servant*** (page 25)
someone whose job is to cook, clean, or do other work in someone else's home.

32 ***occasion*** (page 25)
a time at which something happens.

33 ***retire*** (page 27)
to stop working, especially when you reach the age when you are officially too old to work.

34 ***tap*** (page 28)
to touch someone or something gently, or to make a soft knocking sound. The man is indicating that he is impatient because Bridget's mother is late.

35 ***suspicious*** (page 28)
believing that someone has probably done something wrong.

36 ***attention*** – *to pay attention to someone/something* (page 29)
to listen to, watch, or consider something or someone very carefully.

37 ***panic*** (page 30)
a sudden strong feeling of fear or worry that makes you unable to think clearly or calmly.

38 ***ice-queen*** (page 32)
a woman who behaves in an unfriendly way and does not show any emotion or interest in other people.

39 ***gorgeous*** (page 32)
very beautiful.

40 ***ignore*** (page 32)
to pretend that you have not noticed someone or something.

41 ***hostess*** (page 35)
a woman who invites someone to a meal or party, or to stay for a short time in her home.

42 ***inner poise*** (page 38)
a controlled and relaxed way of behaving, even in difficult situations.

43 ***chat show*** (page 38)
a television or radio programme in which people talk about themselves and their work.

44 ***grab*** (page 42)
to take hold of something in a rough or rude way.

45 ***pregnant*** (page 45)
if a woman is pregnant, she has a baby developing inside her body.

46 ***concentrate*** (page 47)
to give all your attention to the thing you are doing.

47 ***idiot*** (page 47)
someone who behaves in a stupid way.
48 ***rat*** (page 49)
someone who is not loyal or who tricks you.
49 ***interrupt*** (page 49)
to make something stop for a period of time.
50 ***opportunity*** (page 51)
a chance to do something, or a situation in which it is easy for you to do something.
51 ***minibreak*** (page 52)
a short holiday for only two or three days.
52 ***cricket*** (page 53)
a game played by two teams of 11 players who get points by hitting a ball with a bat and running between two sets of sticks called stumps.
53 ***persuade*** (page 53)
to make someone agree to do something by giving them reasons why they should.
54 ***bear*** (page 54)
if you cannot bear something, you cannot accept or do it because it makes you very unhappy.
55 ***bikini*** (page 55)
a swimming suit for women, with separate parts to cover the breasts and the lower part of the body.
56 ***fancy dress party*** (page 57)
a party where people wear clothes that make them look like a famous person, an animal, a character from a story etc. Clothes that you wear at a fancy dress party are called a *costume*.
57 ***firm*** (page 57)
showing that you are in control of a situation and will not be easily forced to do something.
58 ***stockings*** (page 58)
a piece of women's clothing that tightly covers the feet and legs. Stockings are attached at the top of the leg to a piece of underwear that has hooks to hold them up.
59 ***bridesmaid*** (page 61)
a girl or young woman who helps a bride before and during her wedding.
60 ***regret*** (page 64)
to feel sorry or sad about something that you have said or done.

61 ***researcher*** (page 66)
someone who does research, especially someone who works for a television or film company collecting relevant facts and ideas.
62 ***current affairs*** (page 66)
political, social, and economic events that are happening now and are discussed in news programmes and newspapers.
63 ***eligible*** (page 67)
considered to be suitable as a marriage partner because you are rich or attractive.
64 ***ruby wedding*** (page 70)
the day when people celebrate 40 years of marriage.
65 ***fireman's pole*** (page 72)
a *pole* is a long thin stick, often used for holding or supporting something. Firemen use a long pole instead of stairs to move quickly from one level of the fire station building to another.
66 ***showy*** (page 75)
big and expensive in a way that seems ugly.
67 ***glamorous*** (page 77)
interesting in an exciting and unusual way.
68 ***trial*** (page 79)
the process of examining a case in a court of law and deciding whether someone is guilty or innocent.
69 ***High Court*** (page 79)
a court of law in the UK that has more power than ordinary courts, and in which previous court decisions can be changed.
70 ***nanny*** (page 79)
a woman whose job is to look after someone else's children. A nanny usually lives with the family that she works for.
71 ***defend*** (page 80)
to be the lawyer in a court case who tries to prove that someone is not guilty.
72 ***dye*** (page 85)
a substance used for changing the colour of something such as clothing or your hair.
73 ***marmalade*** (page 85)
a sweet food made from cooked fruit such as oranges or lemons that is usually spread onto bread and eaten at breakfast.

74 ***time-share*** (page 86)
a flat or house that you buy with other people so that you can each use it for a particular amount of time every year.

75 ***remortgage*** (page 86)
a *mortgage* is a legal agreement in which you borrow money from a bank in order to buy a house. If you *remortgage*, you borrow more money or change the payment arrangements of an existing mortgage.

76 ***ashamed*** (page 88)
feeling guilty or embarrassed because you have done something wrong, or think that you have not reached a standard that people expect.

77 ***helmet*** (page 88)
a hard hat that you wear to protect your head.

78 ***authorities*** (page 90)
the police or people in other official organizations with legal power to make people obey laws or rules.

79 ***planning permission*** (page 90)
official permission from local government to make changes to the structure of a building, or to build a new one.

80 ***French windows*** (page 95)
a pair of glass doors that lead to a garden.

Exercises

Background

Choose the correct information to complete the sentences. The first one is an example.

1 The author of *Bridget Jones's Diary* is English / American.

2 Helen Fielding wrote *Bridget Jones's Diary* while she was working as a journalist / publishing assistant.

3 The novel *Bridget Jones's Diary* was published in 1995 / 1996.

4 Bridget Jones was popular because she was a beautiful heroine / likeable woman.

5 Helen Fielding wrote / refused to write a sequel to *Bridget Jones's Diary*.

6 Helen Fielding's husband has worked on *The Simpsons* / *Notting Hill*.

7 *Bridget Jones's Diary* is / is not a true story about the life of Helen Fielding.

8 *Bridget Jones's Diary* shows that women should avoid / enjoy being single.

9 Helen Fielding's *Bridget Jones's Diary* and Jane Austen's *Pride and Prejudice* have similar publication dates / plots.

10 In the film version of the book, Bridget Jones is played by a British / an American actress.

11 Helen Fielding wrote the screenplays for the Bridget Jones films alone / with somebody else.

12 Bridget Jones is in her twenties / thirties.

Vocabulary: opposites in context

Choose the best OPPOSITE (a–d) of the underlined word/phrase from the story. The first one is done for you.

1 'Perpetua was wearing a tight red skirt, which made her bottom look very big' (p14)
a long **b** fashionable **c** loose **d** patterned

2 'She sat down in front of the mirror and put on her eye make-up' (p30)
a put off **b** took off **c** took out **d** turned off

3 'Her skin was clear and her hair was shining' (p30)
a bright **b** dull **c** untidy **d** heavy

4 'For a moment neither of us spoke' (p12)
a all **b** both **c** some **d** none

5 'Oh God. I'll be sacked' (p80)
a fired **b** hired **c** retired **d** unemployed

6 'Your skirt is clearly absent. Is skirt off sick?' (p16)
a away **b** well **c** recent **d** here

7 'Then he whispered, 'This is just a bit of fun, OK?'' (p20)
a spoke **b** shouted **c** asked **d** mentioned

Grammar: present perfect simple/continuous

Choose the best verb form (present perfect simple or present perfect continuous) to complete the sentences. The first one is an example.

1 Daniel has gone / has been going to a meeting in Croydon and he'll be back tomorrow.

2 I've called / I've been calling Mum and Dad all week, but there's still no answer.

3 I've booked / I've been booking a nice hotel for a minibreak next weekend and I hope that Daniel is going to like it.

4 At the New Year's Day party I asked Mark, '<u>Have you stayed / Have you been staying</u> with your parents over New Year?'

5 <u>I've wasted / I've been wasting</u> the whole day getting ready for a date with Daniel, which he <u>has just cancelled / has just been cancelling</u>.

6 My mother <u>has never presented / has never been presenting</u> a television show before.

7 <u>I've watched / I've been watching</u> the Elena Rossini interview five times so far.

Vocabulary: expressions with *get*

Choose the best expression with 'get' from the box below to complete each sentence. You may need to change the tense or form of the verb. The first one is done for you.

~~get drunk~~	get back	get ready	
get in touch	get serious	get stuck	get divorced

1 Bridget thinks that her life is empty because she always goes out and ......*gets drunk*...... in bars.

2 In the changing rooms, Bridget's dress .... as she tries to take it off.

3 Jude's boyfriend thinks that she is .... about their relationship because she wants to go on holiday with him.

4 Mark Darcy talks to Julio and manages to .... some of the stolen money.

5 Una tells Mark to take Bridget's phone number so he can .... with her in London.

6 Bridget spends time learning about current affairs in order to .... for her interview.

7 Bridget's mother tells her that Mark Darcy has just .... and is now an eligible bachelor.

Vocabulary: adjectives of feeling

Complete the adjectives which describe the characters' feelings in the story. The first three letters of each adjective are given. The first one is an example.

1 Bridget feels **lon***ely*.................... when she thinks she is the only one not having fun at Christmas.

2 Bridget is **sho**.................... when she first sees her mother on TV.

3 Bridget and her father think her mother should feel **ash**.................... when she arrives back in England, because Julio stole her friends' money.

4 Bridget is **emb**.................... when everyone at the Alconburys' party stares at her after she talks too quickly to Mark Darcy.

5 Bridget says that starting a new job is very tiring. She feels completely **exh**.................... at the end of her first day.

6 Bridget gets **ups**.................... when she thinks she is pregnant and Shazzer has to calm her down.

7 Bridget wants to cook a delicious dinner for her friends and she is **dis**.................... when the meal is not a big success.

8 Everyone feels very **gra**.................... to Mark Darcy when he manages to make a deal with Julio and get some of their money back.

9 Bridget feels **mis**.................... when Daniel does not ask her on a date at the weekend, and she calls Shazzer to tell her how bad her life is.

10 Bridget is **sus**.................... about her mother's relationship with Julio – is this the reason for her parents' problems?

11 Bridget starts to feel **jea**.................... of her mother having a relationship with Julio while she herself is single.

12 Bridget feels **con**.................... by Daniel's behaviour towards her. She cannot understand why sometimes he wants to be with her and at other times he ignores her.

Sentence transformations: *I wonder / I'd like to know / I want to know…*

Rewrite the sentences to describe what Bridget is thinking, using *I wonder / I'd like to know / I want to know …* at the beginning. The first one is an example.

1 'Is Daniel Cleaver attracted to me?'
I wonder *if Daniel Cleaver is attracted to me.*

2 'Why has Dad started ringing up in the night?'
I wonder

3 'Why do my parents' friends always have to ask me when I'm getting married?'
I'd like to know

4 'Is the Valentine's Day card for me or Vanessa?'
I wonder

5 'Should I tell Magda that her husband is having an affair?'
I wonder

6 'Does Dad know about Julio?'
I wonder

7 'Why hasn't Rebecca invited me to her party?'
I want to know

8 'When is Mum coming back from Portugal?'
I'd like to know

Vocabulary: verbs and nouns

a **Match a verb with a noun to make phrases from the story. The first one is done for you.**

1 make	weight
2 put on	a tax form
3 ring	no notice
4 fill in	a cigarette
5 pay	a deal
6 take	attention
7 light	the doorbell

b **Now choose phrases from a to complete the sentences below, changing the tense or form of the verb where necessary. Each phrase may only be used once. The first one is an example.**

1 Mark ....*made a deal*........ with Julio to get back some of the money that he had stolen from Bridget's parents' friends.

2 A man who knew about money helped Bridget's mother to ....

3 Bridget decided to .... of Daniel when he returned from America. By ignoring him, she knew she would make him .... to her.

4 Bridget did not hear Mark when he .... because she was using a noisy hairdryer.

5 Daniel took a match and ...., before calling room service.

6 Bridget always counted the calories in everything she ate because she was worried about ....

Making questions

Write the questions for the answers shown.

Example: *Who wrote 'Bridget Jones's Diary'?*
Helen Fielding wrote 'Bridget Jones's Diary'.

Q1 *Who*

A1 It's Daniel Cleaver who sends Bridget email messages about her skirt.

Q2 *Whose*

A2 Jude's partner is known to her friends as 'Vile Richard'.

Q3 *Where*

A3 Bridget has to go to the fire station to interview firemen.

Q4 *How*

A4 Bridget weighs 8st 12 on 18 June.

Q5 *What*

A5 Bridget dreams of going on a romantic minibreak with Daniel.

Q6 *Why*

A6 The soup turns blue because Bridget puts bright blue string in the water.

Q7 *Why*

A7 Mark Darcy had helped Bridget's family because he loved her.

Q8 *How*

A8 Bridget kept one of her New Year's resolutions.

Published by Macmillan Heinemann ELT
Between Towns Road, Oxford OX4 3PP
A division of Macmillan Publishers Limited
Companies and representatives throughout the world
Heinemann is the registered trademark of Pearson Education, used under licence.

ISBN 978–0–2307–3120–2
ISBN 978–0–2307–1670–4 (with CD pack)

This version of *Bridget Jones's Diary* by Helen Fielding was retold by Anne Collins for Macmillan Readers

First published 2009

This version first published 2009

Illustrated by Gavin Reece
Cover by Rex Features

Printed and bound in Thailand

2014 2013 2012 2011 2010 2009
10 9 8 7 6 5 4 3 2 1

with CD pack
2014 2013 2012 2011 2010 2009
10 9 8 7 6 5 4 3 2 1